Josephine & Napoleon

Margaret Laing

'Those persons who were not acquainted with the Empress Josephine will find my account of her in some degree exaggerated; those, on the contrary, who have been attached to her household will very justly observe that I have kept within the truth.'

> Lady-in-Waiting to the Duchess of Navarre

'If Josephine had been my mother, my father would never have been sent to St Helena and I would not be wasting away here in Vienna.'

> The King of Rome, Napoleon Bonaparte II

Frontispiece – The Empress Josephine by Gros. The painting hangs at Malmaison

Librairie Hachette

1

Josephine & Napoleon

Margaret Laing

SIDGWICK & JACKSON
LONDON

Other books by Margaret Laing
ROBERT KENNEDY
WOMAN ON WOMAN (ed.)
EDWARD HEATH: PRIME MINISTER

To my mother, who had the idea

First published in Great Britain in 1973
Copyright © 1973 Margaret Laing
ISBN 0 283 98105 9

Design by Bob Burroughs
Picture research by Mary Dru

Photoset by Typesetting Services, Glasgow and
Printed in Great Britain by
William Clowes & Sons, Limited
London, Beccles and Colchester
for Sidgwick & Jackson Limited
1 Tavistock Chambers, Bloomsbury Way
London WC1A 2SG

Contents

1. Seven in the Morning

7 in the morning

I awake full of you. Your portrait and the thought of the intoxication of last night have given my senses no rest.

Sweet and incomparable Josephine, what a bizarre effect you have upon my heart. Are you angry? Do I see you sad? Are you worried? My heart is broken, and there is no respite for your friend . . . But how much more so when, abandoning myself to this passion that rules me, I drink a burning flame from your lips and from your heart. Oh! This night has shown me that your portrait is not you!

You leave at noon; in three hours I shall see you. Meanwhile, *mio dolce amor*, a thousand kisses; but do not give me any, for they set my blood on fire.

NB

Seven o'clock on a December morning in Paris in 1795, dark and cold, when most people except servants and the young general who was writing this letter were still in bed. He was twenty-six, and as yet little-known. He normally rose very early, but this morning was different. A few hours earlier his burning passion for a woman of the world six years his senior, a widow with a teenage son and a daughter had met success, and been further inflamed. He was a Corsican, proud, poor, lonely and intense. She was not formally beautiful, but evocative, the essence of sympathy, generous. And the first woman to give him confidence in himself.

They had met barely two months before: but this night was crucial, and they were never to be really free of each other for the next nineteen years. This night probably changed the course of French history and led indirectly, in default of a mature heir to the Empire, to the Bourbon restoration of 1814.

For the moment the soldier was only conscious of how long the three hours seemed till he would meet this fascinating woman again. He could not know that for and through each

Photo Bulloz

*Josephine when she was
young, and still called
Rose*

Martinique: the sucrerie
*in which raw sugar was
produced on the family
plantation. The Taschers
moved in to live on the
upper floor after a hurricane destroyed their house*

Roger-Viollet

other they were to suffer terribly, yet at times to achieve perfect love and peace. In the kiln of their relationship, she was to mature and mellow, he to harden and nearly to crack.

Outwardly they were oddly assorted, not only in age but, particularly under the microscope of French society, in social graces, of which she had so many and he, almost deliberately it seemed, so few. Yet temperamentally they possessed in common many qualities which they found in few others – loyalty, a natural sense of justice, and above all a capacity for feeling. The great leveller, the Revolution, had seen them both imprisoned at different times: death had seemed close, but had slipped quietly past them. Now they were left with a hunger for the future.

When the time came, in exile, for him to look back on that future, he said, 'She was the most alluring, most glamorous creature I have ever known. A woman in the full sense of the word – changeable, spirited, and with the kindest of hearts.' As such, he had crowned her beside him, Empress of France.

Neither Napoleon nor Josephine was born on the mainland of France, and, surprisingly, though both could charm with and without words, neither of them ever learnt to speak without the accents which proclaimed their island births – his in Corsica, hers on the tropical rum and sugar island of Martinique, facing Central America across the Caribbean. She had a Créole accent, a slight drawl, which had a fascination for those used to the precision of Parisian French, enhanced by the particular quality of her voice itself, low and mellifluous.

The French word 'Créole' of the time did not indicate mixed blood, but on the contrary someone of pure French or Spanish blood, born and bred in the colonies – particularly those in the tropics. Josephine's father, Joseph-Gaspard Tascher de la Pagerie, who was indolent and not much of a family man – in both these respects the very opposite of her second husband, Napoleon – was a struggling sugar-planter. As was suggested by the 'de' in his name, he had noble blood: the family could trace its name back to the twelfth century, when they had lived in the Loire valley. Josephine's great-grandfather had emigrated from Orléans in 1726, hoping to make his fortune in the West Indies, but neither he nor his descendants were gifted at making or keeping money, which was the chief occupation and preoccupation of most people on the island. The best thing that Joseph-Gaspard had been able to achieve since he returned from five years at the French Court (an honour due to his lineage: he served the Dauphine Marie-Louise, mother of Louis XVI, who was now on the throne) was marriage to a spinster of twenty-five, only one year younger than himself. But she, too, had noble blood, and, more important, she had assets of her own.

It was on the bride's sugar plantation, with its 150 slaves, its acres of cane, its admixture of mules, goats, sheep, and cows, its wooden house, and its big solid stone sugar refinery, that the couple lived – or at least the wife. Her husband spent more and more time away from her in Fort-Royal, the capital (now Fort-de-France). She hoped that an heir would revive her husband's desire for her, if this had ever existed. But the birth of a girl at the beginning of the rainy season, on 23 June 1763, produced mixed feelings in her: 'Contrary to all our wishes, God has chosen to give us a daughter. My joy has been no less great . . . Why should we not have a more favourable view of our own sex? I know some who combine so many good qualities that it would seem impossible to find them all in any other person.' Many would think the same about the child in later years. At five weeks she was baptized Marie-Josèphe-Rose; thirty-two years later Napoleon would re-name her Josephine.

As can be glimpsed from her letters and was asserted by her contemporaries, Josephine's mother was an intelligent, resolute woman. Two more pregnancies raised her hopes for a son and an increase in her husband's regard: but the result was two more daughters. Their father was not all bad, but even his brother could see his faults. 'He means well,' he wrote. 'He loves his family, above all his children, but he must be pushed.'

Just before the birth of her youngest sister, the three-year-old Josephine had her first glimpse of terror, the first in a life that was to be shot through with terrible experiences.

Martinique was a beautiful island: it was hot, luxuriant, gaudy with tropical flowers, orchids, bougainvillaea, jasmine, scarlet flambeau trees, hibiscus, redolent of honeysuckle and amaryllis, with tropical birds in brilliant plumage flashing past the tangled creepers and the tall palms and banana trees. But it was not a very secure island. It was frequently a target for the Dutch and British, and had in fact been returned to France by Britain only a year before Josephine's birth. It also had its natural dangers: frequent earthquakes and a volcano were the most dreaded, but there were the daily dangers from snakes and mosquitoes, and the year that Josephine was born there had been a gigantic invasion of ants that had eaten its way across the island, devouring crops, corpses, snakes, all that lay in its path. Josephine had to be guarded in her cradle by slaves.

However, the island did have a reputation for being remarkably free, by the standards of the West Indies, from hurricanes.

Then on 13 August 1766 one of the Caraib chiefs came to tell the household that he had seen warning signs of a storm. The tocsin, or alarm, was rung, and the family, with the mulatto nurse Marion holding Josephine, took shelter in the sugar refinery, while fishes left the sea to flee up-river, and birds sought refuge with humans.

Contemporary records are contradictory: but by the next morning between 400 and 1,600 people had died; eighty ships had been sunk – the cabin-boy from one survived when the wind carried him from the sinking deck to dry land – and in one town ninety people were buried alive.

When the family looked out they found that, apart from its sturdy stone kitchen, the wooden house had vanished. From now on they would live in the upper floor of the refinery.

Another blow to the family finances came with the death of Josephine's grandfather on her mother's side. He had expected to leave a substantial sum of money but instead left debts. A secure future as the promised bride of one of the rich Martinique planters – many girls were married at thirteen or fourteen – could no longer be assured for Josephine, who would have no dowry.

But the everyday needs of life were plentifully supplied: the

Photo Bulloz

Carlo Bonaparte, Napoleon's father, was a likable lawyer who enjoyed spending money on clothes

The house where Napoleon was born in Ajaccio

Photo Bulloz

shortage was of cash and luxuries, not of food, warmth and slaves. As she grew older Josephine slept in a pretty little four-poster bed made from the wood of locust trees. By the time Napoleon was born she was six, and teaching her younger sisters the names and colours of all the plants and wild creatures of the island; just as after the hurricane she never lost her terror of high winds, so she never lost her love for Martinique, and this would benefit Europe later when she began to import tropical birds and flowers into France. She loved them almost passionately.

At ten, her four years' of formal education began. She went to the convent of Les Dames de la Providence, but her real education, simple as it was, took place at home.

Josephine, the eldest of three girls, two of whom were to die young, was a peace-maker and lover of peace all her life. Sweetness, goodness and generosity were qualities that began to emerge as definite characteristics when she was still a child. She could not bear to see the slaves punished, in accordance with the savage practices still allowed under the *Code Noir* drawn up by Louis XIV, which meant flogging and branding with the fleur de lis for the illegal assembly of slaves from different owners, loss of an ear and a shoulder brand for running away for more than a month, and death for any assault which caused a contusion or effusion of blood. She regarded the slaves she knew best as her friends, in later years would always ask in her letters to be remembered to them all, and gave her own nurse Marion and some others their freedom. The slaves loved her too: a fact that was to have great significance when she married.

How different was the island society in which Napoleon was reared. He was born in Corsica in August 1769 to a happily married couple who were certainly far from polished in the ways of the *ancien régime*.

The second son in a family of eight surviving children, he was affectionate and proud even as a child, and refused to cry when he was chastised. He grew even more ambitious, power-hungry and warlike with age, but he, too, loved domestic peace. He always felt that he had enjoyed a happy childhood, and

The earliest known picture of Napoleon, drawn by a fellow student at Brienne

Photo Bulloz

Laure Permon (later Laure Junot, since she married one of Napoleon's generals, and eventually became the Duchess d'Abrantès) remembered times in France when he would sit and tell stories about the island with her mother, also a Corsican, and other friends. 'Bonaparte liked this way of passing an evening,' she said. 'He spoke French very badly, yet everyone listened to him with delight.'

Like Josephine, Napoleon had a mother who was more resolute and managed affairs better than his father. Letizia was a handsome woman of Neapolitan extraction, almost illiterate, who had married at about fourteen. His father Carlo, a charming but spendthrift lawyer, was well-born in Corsican terms, and because he could claim some noble blood was eventually able to obtain scholarships for his second son to one of the Royal Military Schools in France. Napoleon's childhood ended when he was nine and went to school in France. There was some Greek blood way back in his father's family, and it was after a Greek saint that he was named Napoleone, pronounced Nabulione in the Corsican-Italian dialect.

Napoleon always said he had left Corsica too early to speak Italian well; and so he never had perfect command of any language in his life. However, at the Royal Military School at Brienne he showed that he was good at mathematics, and fair at geography and history.

The lessons he would never forget, however, were those he had learned from Letizia. Even when he was in exile on St Helena these came back to him vividly. He told General Bertrand: 'In my family it was a matter of principle with us not to spend money. We never bought anything that wasn't strictly necessary, such as clothes, furniture. But we spent practically nothing on food . . . The family owned a communal mill to which all the villagers brought their flour to be milled, and they paid for this with a certain percentage of flour. We also had a communal bakehouse, the use of which was paid for in fish . . . The main thing was not to have to part with a penny. Money was very scarce . . . It was a point of honour with my family that we never bought any bread, oil or wine.' Like Josephine's family, then, his had credit but not cash.

14

Letizia's dour outlook provided France with one of its greatest historical comments, voiced in her harsh Corsican accent, when he became Emperor – '*Pourvue que çela doure*' (provided that it lasts). When she visited her son at court she brought with her one cotton dress for a ten-day stay. One of her daughters, Pauline, remonstrated with her, but she called the girl an 'extravagant gipsy', and said she must save against future family misfortune. Napoleon was irritated by her tacit refusal to enjoy the fruits of his success, and to lead an out-going social life, and though he remembered her precepts he probably loved Josephine the more for being free from such inhibitions.

Honour and money were both of prime importance in this rather crude society; if the family was Italian by extraction it was distinctly Corsican in its pride and, with the exception of Napoleon himself, in its gift for carrying on feuds. In later years the whole family, with the exception of the Emperor, would wage war relentlessly on Josephine. Corsica was the birth-place of the blood-feud, or vendetta, to be pursued until no member, even a child, of the hated clan still lived: this has been true even within living memory.

In peasant Corsica, women held a very lowly position. They were kept almost in purdah, perhaps because of the years of Moorish domination. In peasant society the men were fed before the females, and two kinds of bread were baked, the inferior kind for the women! Napoleon was always contemptuous of women in the political sphere, when he might have done well to take Josephine's advice.

As a boy Napoleon thought of himself as Corsican, not French. The island was, in fact, only ceded to France by the Genoese the year before he was born. His father Carlo had for a time supported the rebel Paoli, who wanted independence for the island. Arriving in France at the age of nine, Napoleon felt that he was looked down upon for being poor and Corsican. As Josephine later told her ladies-in-waiting, the other students taunted him when he worked hard 'You Corsican dog . . . you only want to gain favour with the masters', to which he replied, 'You will see what a Corsican can do'. But even ice in his pitcher

15

at Brienne caused trouble. He remembered that when he demanded 'Who has been putting ice in my pitcher?', 'Everyone laughed and made fun of me'. Then the supervisor came up and said, 'Why do you make fun of Monsieur? He comes from a country where there is never any ice.'

When Napoleon started his senior schooling at the age of nine, Josephine, then fifteen, had left her convent more than a year before. While he was starting to explore mathematics and burying himself in a burrow of books that ranged from Boswell's *Account of Corsica* to all the works of Rousseau, some of which aroused in him such strong feelings of disagreement that he committed them to paper, while he was feeling most lonely and at his adolescent lowest, Josephine was beginning to bloom for the first time as a young woman, and facing her first great personal crisis.

In her four years at school she had learned to read, write, embroider, dance, and sing a little in her charming voice. The lack of academic training among Créole ladies was ridiculed in Paris; but Martinique was a law unto itself. Knowledge was not very highly prized; courtesy was. The approach to the intellect was *laissez-aller*, but the approach to all the charms and graces of comfortable life was the opposite. With a father who had served at court, and a mother who loved her three daughters dearly, and had the highest hopes for them in spite of their lack of dowries, the girls had been encouraged to make the best of their natural charms.

On their father's side the children had an uncle, the Baron Tascher, and an Aunt Edmée (formally baptized Marie-Euphémie-Desirée), who in 1757, at the age of twenty, was strikingly beautiful. This was the year, six years before Josephine's birth, when a new governor of the Windward Islands of America had arrived to take up his post in Martinique. He was the Marquis of Beauharnais, a married man, and he engaged the beautiful Edmée as *dame de compagnie* (companion) to his wife. She became godmother to his younger son, Alexandre, who was born in 1760, and who was to be Josephine's first husband.

Edmée soon became the governor's mistress (and, many

"My life is a perpetual nightmare"—letter from Napoleon, in Italy, to Josephine, 1796

years later, his wife). When the governor was recalled to France, Edmée (who meantime had married and almost immediately separated from a highly unsatisfactory husband) sailed with him and his wife, but three-year-old Alexandre, who was considered too young for the journey, was left in the care of Josephine's family at Trois Ilets. He rejoined his parents, and his godmother, when he was five and Josephine two.

When Viscount Alexandre became interested in women, Edmée suggested that he might marry one of her nieces. Marriage for him would have the advantage of giving him his inheritance at once, at seventeen, instead of at twenty-one; if it was to one of her own family, Edmée perhaps felt, she would benefit both her brother's family and her godson, and strengthen her links with the Marquis.

She had for a long time tried to persuade her brother to send Josephine to Paris to be educated; Josephine lived for the idea, but Joseph-Gaspard had never had the money. Now, when a letter suggesting the marriage arrived at the plantation, a further blow fell: for the daughter chosen was not Josephine, but Catherine-Desirée, one year younger. The Marquis of

Beauharnais explained: 'My son, who is only seventeen and a half, finds that a young lady of fifteen is of an age too close to his own.' (Actually, that October 1777 Josephine was only fourteen years and four months old!)

But Josephine, who later showed a jealous though not an envious streak, had no possible chance to resent this proposal to her sister: Catherine-Desirée had died from a fever on 16 October exactly one week before the letter was sent from Noisy-le-Grand, near Paris.

The blow to this affectionate family, in which only the father seemed sometimes an outsider, must have had deep reverberations. But the practicalities of life were carried on with new intensity. Which of the other sisters would Alexandre choose?

Joseph-Gaspard, taking the hint that Josephine was too old, suggested the eleven-and-a-half-year-old Marie-Françoise. Alexandre told Aunt Edmée that the alternative 'seems to me quite natural'. However, the child herself, hardly surprisingly, dreaded the thought of leaving home and her mother, and a few months later her father wrote again, saying that she had been ill, and that 'They [a pronoun which hints at a strong alliance between his wife and her mother] even blame the three months' fever that she has just suffered on her fear that I should force her into it'.

In the interim he had written another letter which showed how the wind was blowing with Josephine. 'The eldest girl, who left the convent some time ago and has for a long time frequently asked me to take her to France, will I fear be somewhat affected by the preference which I appear to give to her younger sister. She has a beautiful skin, beautiful eyes, beautiful arms . . .'

When the youngest girl's reluctance to go turned to repugnance, he wrote that Josephine was still consumed with desire to come to France, and to see her aunt. 'They have tried to put her on her guard also but . . . she is more reasonable.' Then, cleverly trying to turn her age to a double advantage, he reminded them that she was only fifteen *today*: 'This age does not seem to be too close to that of the chevalier;

she is also well-developed for her age and has grown to such an extent in the last five or six months that one could take her for at least eighteen . . .'

Before this letter even arrived the Marquis had written arbitrarily: 'She whom you think best suited to my son will be the one that we desire; be on your way and let us know which of the two you are bringing.'

So it was Josephine's eagerness and her little sister's reluctance that turned the scales. It was not until August 1778 that Joseph-Gaspard could get passages for himself, Josephine, and her mulatto maid Euphémie, whose freedom she was later to obtain.

Josephine knew that she was to marry a Viscount of seventeen, of whom she had heard glowing descriptions from her aunt, his godmother. Beyond that, she knew little of what she could expect. Had she had a little more knowledge of the world, she might have guessed at least something from Alexandre's sudden startling reference to herself in a letter as the 'elder daughter whom we have always desired more ardently than the younger'.

With a little more age and experience, Josephine's natural sensitivity and her acquired knowledge of people *in extremis* and in the highest seats of power would give her an almost intuitive accuracy in understanding character, and thus in predicting the fortunes of others. But as someone who usually remained essentially passive, she saw herself more as someone buffeted by the storms of life than as in control of her own destiny. This made her superstitious; and she had had her fortune told by a Negro soothsayer in Martinique.

Napoleon and the daughter later born to her both affirm that she was told she would marry young, be unhappy, be widowed, and later become 'more than Queen' of France. To this one of her last and youngest ladies-in-waiting, Mlle Ducrest, adds that the Empress remembered the prediction ending 'you will enjoy many years of happiness, but you will be killed in a popular commotion'. Only one part of the prophecy did not come true.

2. Married to a Bachelor

The sixteen-year-old Josephine married her nineteen-year-old bridegroom on 13 December 1779. Over the next fifteen years of marriage she was to spend fewer than fifteen months with her husband; and fewer still of these would be happy.

Alexandre's first glimpse of her came six weeks before they were married, on 27 October, a fortnight after she had disembarked at Brest exhausted from her voyage. Always a bad traveller, throughout her life Josephine was to suffer considerably, both physically and emotionally, from such journeys. A person who needed deep roots, she was easily homesick: but apart from her family, she was not homesick for Martinique; it was France, to which she had looked forward for so long with intoxicated expectations, that always held her heart.

The young Viscount's first impression of her was cool and objective; the foundation on which the future Empress built her fascination was this: 'Mlle Tascher', he wrote to his father, 'will perhaps appear to you less pretty than you had expected, but I think I may assure you that the honesty and sweetness [*l'honnêteté et la douceur*] of her nature will surpass what you have been told.'

Though she did not yet know it, Josephine was facing the reverse in her husband. Her future letters would show that she had considered herself in love with him. He was fairly good-looking, and was judged 'one of the most attractive gentlemen of his time'. Elegant, self-centred, a good dancer, he had been educated largely by a tutor, Patricol, and had then accompanied Patricol when he was engaged to instruct the two nephews of the Duke of Rochefoucauld. The Duke himself was intelligently liberal. Alexandre picked up a smattering of modern ideas, and, like many younger sons of the nobility (the very sons who, jealous of their elder brothers, later joined the revolutionaries), became a great snob. However, his lineage was not sufficiently distinguished for him to be able to hunt with Louis XVI, and this, reported his friend Bouillé, was 'a torture to his vanity'.

Josephine swiftly became a second torture to his vanity. She fell painfully short of his short-sighted demands. It was not her

20   *The Viscount Alexandre de Beauharnais, Josephine's first husband*

Photo Bulloz

looks that worried him: she was very pleasant-looking if not beautiful. Her hair was chestnut-brown, her eyes changed constantly in colour but were probably hazel, her complexion was a little darker than was fashionable in Paris, and, in spite of her beautiful arms, she probably had a little puppy fat – Alexandre remarked on her 'plump little cheeks'. Two passport descriptions from later years give the cursory facts: 'height five feet, nose and mouth well made, eyes orange, hair and eyebrows dark brown, face long, chin somewhat prominent'; and 'height five feet, eyes dark, hair chestnut, mouth small, chin round, forehead medium, nose small'. She was actually fairly tall for the time, as the contemporary French measure of five feet today equals five feet four inches.

Nor was Alexandre, after the first meeting, greatly concerned with her sweetness. It has her naïveté and her mind that made him blush. Society was greatly amused by anything unusual, and a Créole education was infallibly absurd: as the Count of Montgaillard put it, 'We were all acquainted with great ladies of that origin who, while retaining a place in the highest society, scarcely knew how to read, much less to write. It was a standing joke . . .'

Treating her as he might a new pony that had to be schooled, the young husband swiftly laid down orders for his bride. She was to have lessons in history and geography, read verse aloud, memorize passages from the finest French plays. She was also to practise letter-writing – to him, as he intended to be away most of the time. He announced his intention of rejoining his regiment four months after they were married, and only returned for a few weeks the following winter, 1780–81, before leaving her to another nine months of married, pregnant loneliness in a dark house in the Rue Thévenot, with only her wedding presents and her father-in-law, the old Marquis, and her Aunt Edmée to keep her company. Alexandre openly admitted he was resuming his 'bachelor life'.

This callous behaviour becomes a little easier to understand when one reads a letter Alexandre sent to his godmother Edmée, in August 1777, just before the marriage negotiations were begun. 'I will not hide it from you: your chevalier has known happiness. He is loved by a charming woman who is the object of all desires in the garrison of Brest and the district.' How flattering it was to his strutting ego. But his emotions were engaged, and at the end of October, while it was being decided which of the Tascher daughters he should marry, he was feeling the 'deepest despair' at the thought of leaving the woman he regarded as 'tender' and 'good'. It is hardly surprising that he could not really care less which girl was sacrificed: after all, both families were in favour of the match, and he would inherit his mother's money sooner.

The object of his love also explains his increasing rejection of Josephine. Coincidentally, his mistress too was a Créole: but with a very different nature. Laure, Mme Longpré, born Marie-Françoise-Laure de Girardin de Montgérald, was twenty-nine and had a small daughter when her young lover of seventeen was admitted to her bed. Their child, a son, was born in 1779, and called Alexandre after both his father, and, coincidentally, Laure's husband.

This unknown woman, of whom Josephine had heard in Martinique, was to prove a deliberately malevolent influence on her young life, and was to wreck her marriage for a spiteful whim.

To Laure, and to the alternating absences and criticisms of her petty tyrant husband, coming on top of the uncertainties of life and happiness in Martinique, can probably be attributed Josephine's desperate sense of insecurity in later life whenever she was separated from anyone, children, husband or lover, she had taken to her heart. The unfair comparisons she endured would also contribute to her deliberate perfection of her attractions when she was older.

But in spite of some tendency to be passive, termed by critics as her 'Créole indolence', Josephine showed on this occasion, as she had done when the unseen bride was being chosen in Martinique, that she had a sound sense of justice. When this was injured she would make an obstinate stand on behalf of others or herself.

Alexandre was extremely put out when this little sixteen-year-old chit, instead of merely obeying his instructions wrote complaining about *his* behaviour. 'Do not poison the pleasure which I take in reading what you say by reproaches', he replied sharply.

The next year he complained to Patricol, his old tutor, that his strategy of withdrawing from his wife while she carried out his plan for her education had misfired. He felt a 'lack of trust' in her. While he would, continued the self-deceiver, much prefer a domestic life, he evidently could not bear what this would entail in reality: 'She wants me to occupy myself in society solely with her; she wants to know what I say, what I do, what I write . . .' Josephine, her husband observed, had become jealous.

From what Patricol said to Aunt Edmée, an impression of the way this showed itself can be gleaned. Josephine, he said, should be made to realize that 'brusqueness and dictatorialness are two bad ways to attract the husband she loved'. Patricol had, in the past, had his own grave doubts about the sincerity of his protégé. He had discovered that Alexandre, as a bachelor, was at least listening avidly to 'garrison adventures' (which he soon, according to his friends and letters, indulged in freely), and he wrote: 'What astounds and greatly displeases me in the young man is the extreme care which he takes to conceal, the ease with which he disguises, the feelings of his heart.'

Now, however, family and tutor made an effort to reconcile the wife of eighteen and the husband of twenty-one. Three months later, in September 1781, Josephine had her first baby: a boy, Eugène. Alexandre, as her lawyers phrased it later, 'kept her faithful company until the moment of her arising out of child-bed'. At the beginning of November Alexandre left to go to Italy, returning the following July. Josephine found he 'seemed enchanted to find himself with her again', and became pregnant again.

Almost at once she discovered that Alexandre, who had detested the idea of overseas service while a bachelor, had applied to become aide-de-camp to the present governor of Martinique. The family was once more split with quarrels, with Edmée taking her niece's side against her godson. Two months after he had returned, Josephine woke one early

Eugène de Beauharnais, Josephine's son

The former Carmelite convent in which Josephine was imprisoned for four months during the Revolution

September morning (1782) and found Alexandre had left in the middle of the night, without a word. A letter informed her that he was going to Brest, and thence to Martinique. Her son was a year old, she was two months pregnant, and alone again.

At the end of October she heard that Laure Longpré was also in Brest, staying with an uncle. She wrote to Alexandre angrily; and Edmée, knowing better than her niece the full details of the affair and its lure for her godson, wrote still more strongly.

Alexandre's letters to Josephine at this period were full of reproaches, followed by apologies and heavy attempts at sentiment, followed by more reproaches. Her letters, though much more graceful in style than her early ones, failed to satisfy him, and he seized any excuse to bully her. Before he set sail he sent this message: 'The boat has just arrived and there is not a single word from you . . . if your inconstancy is inevitable, leave me in no doubt about it, so that I need never see you again. Farewell! Excuse this letter but I am in a fury.'

To this and to subsequent letters Josephine did not reply, perhaps because of what she heard next.

Laure had booked a passage on the same boat to Martinique. Alexandre's next letter, from Fort-Royal, told the seven months pregnant Josephine that they had spent their time together on board 'playing ludo', and added, 'I was bored by the game but more than recompensed by the pleasure I received from the company.'

Josephine's family, knowing nothing of these latest troubles (though her father had returned with an account of the early difficulties less than a year before), welcomed Alexandre as one of them during his one and a half day visit to the plantation. He apparently found Joseph-Gaspard, racked with malaria now, at work making sugar. Then he returned to Fort-Royal, to his post as aide-de-camp to the governor, and to Laure.

On 10 April 1783 Josephine's second child was born, a daughter, Hortense. The young mother, still only nineteen, sent her family in Martinique the news; but she did not write to inform her husband. He had forfeited almost the last of her hurt feelings for him, and in a letter to her Aunt Rosette she said she had got over the lively feeling her husband had once aroused in her.

It was the birth of this beloved baby girl, who, with her brother Eugène, was to bring Josephine all the joy she knew in her twenties, and like him was to be one great source of happiness for her as long as she lived, that precipitated the final crisis and misery.

Alexandre was delighted by the news of the birth. While he was receiving congratulations in the Fort-Royal salon of the demoiselles Hurault, Laure coldly and loudly pointed out that the child had been born less than nine months after his return from Italy. It could not be his, since everyone knew that babies might be born late, but never early.

Laure was shortly to return to Paris to marry her second husband, Count Dillon. It therefore seems that her action was not motivated even by possessiveness, but simply by spite, an extraordinary malevolence considering that she was in possession of the child's father at that very moment.

Alexandre was possessed by an immature and egotistical fury. First of all, inspired probably by Laure, the pair set out on a frenzied hunt for any scurrilous evidence they could produce against the child Josephine. They interrogated the slaves on the plantation, offered them money to talk or to corroborate the idea of a depraved adolescence, threatened their lives if they should report their questions to the family. If was four years since Josephine had left the island, but her genuine affection for the slaves now had its reward in their loyalty to her: Brigitte, her former maid, was vehement in her defence; Alexandre offered money to a boy who was only five when she left Martinique, and failed again. Finally, for a large sum, he managed to bribe a third slave, Maximin, to corroborate his suspicions (he was later, as her mother wrote to Josephine, 'put on the chain', though well fed), but for the moment Mme Tascher told her daughter nothing about the allegations that had been made against her, no doubt hoping that such manufactured slanders would die a natural death.

The first Josephine knew of the final unhappiness that was brewing was when Laure herself visited her at Noisy-le-Grand

27

in late summer. She brought with her a letter from Alexandre dated 12 July 1783, which informed Josephine, 'in my eyes you are the vilest of creatures'.

The incredible Alexandre continued: 'A being who could, while preparing to leave [Martinique], take a lover in her arms when she knows she is destined for another, has no soul: she is lower than all the jades [*coquines*] in the world...' As for the baby Hortense, he said, he might be forced to accept her, but he knew that 'a stranger's blood flows in her veins'. Therefore, he requested icily, 'have the goodness to take yourself to a convent as soon as this letter arrives. This is my last word...I must warn you that you would find me a tyrant if you did not punctually follow what I have said.'

An example of Josephine's extreme forbearance was her virtual forgiveness of her husband later; still more striking was a note in which, as Empress, she asked Napoleon to sanction a pension for Laure, explaining simply 'this lady is now very infirm'.

But for the moment, at twenty, her reaction must simply have been one of bewilderment and shock. She was never able to hide her feelings or the cause of them, and perhaps the surest refutation of the charges – which Alexandre himself later publicly withdrew – was the spontaneous and united support given to her by both sides of the family, the Beauharnais – the Marquis, and Alexandre's aunt, uncle, brother, and sister-in-law – as well as the Taschers. A second letter, dated October, expressed astonishment that she was not yet immured in a convent. Alexandre sent this after returning to France, but refused to see his wife. Finally, in November, she retired to the convent of Penthémont in the Rue de Grenelle. The baby Hortense had to be left with a wet-nurse, but two-year-old Eugène and Aunt Edmée accompanied Josephine: for this convent, in which one could rent pleasant apartments very reasonably, was in fact a very fashionable 'staging post' for well-bred women who found themselves in domestic difficulties, while their future was smoothed out.

Relying no doubt on her aunt's advice (which came from the experience of a separation from her own husband in the early days of her relationship with the Marquis), Josephine had legal advice within two weeks. She applied not for a divorce, but for a separation. The father of one of her advocates met her, and his description (to his wife) shows how much she had changed in the four years or so since her marriage: 'a fascinating young person, a lady of distinction and elegance, with perfect style, a multitude of graces and the most beautiful of speaking voices.' What an evocative description this is: and yet it contains not one word about Josephine's appearance.

The swan was beginning to emerge, and was nurtured by the elegance, fashion, and personal gifts of the cultivated society around her. Outwardly Josephine was a great imitator, and learned all she knew from observation and conversation. Inwardly, she never learned to harden her heart to match the self-imprisoning brilliance of the *ancien régime*.

Just over a year after she had entered the convent, Alexandre capitulated, although, according to contemporary French law, he still had eighteen months in which to go on searching for any shred of evidence to support his accusations. Josephine's terms, which the Viscount now readily accepted, allowed her to live where she pleased and to run her own affairs, to receive an allowance from him, to keep Eugène until he was five (and afterwards during holidays) and Hortense until she married. In her circumstances, this amounted to having all the advantages of marriage to Alexandre with none of the disadvantages.

She was so comfortable in the convent that she chose to stay there for another six months. Then, late in 1785, aged twenty-two, she came out into the world again to join her Aunt Edmée and the Marquis in a house that Edmée had rented at Fontainebleau. Unlike the naïve girl who had been introduced to society six years before, this was her real debut: she knew now what was expected of a viscountess. She moved in a wider and even more fashionable circle than before, apparently enjoying life, whether this consisted of looking after her children or returning soaked to the skin after following Louis XVI all day on a boar hunt. (She enjoyed the chase, but could not bear to see animals caught and killed. Later, when Napoleon had time to hunt, she would beg him to cancel the arrange-

29

ments when the animals were carrying their young.) On such exhilarating days none of them could possibly know how short a future this phase of their lives would have; nor that the hardships they themselves hardly even glimpsed would lead to the Revolution in only four years.

In 1788 Josephine decided to take Hortense to Martinique. The trip, which lasted nearly three years, was the only return visit she would ever make to her birth-place. Those who had waved goodbye to her nine years before must have been astonished when she stepped ashore again by her greater dignity, polish, and poise, though her social delicacy had its roots in the extreme courtesy of their own ways. From Hortense herself, who was only five when she first saw Martinique, we have some glimpses of the woman seen by those who knew her well: her emotional vividness, her vulnerability, her loyalty – quite simply, her tremendous and unrestrained capacity for feeling.

Hardly had they set sail when, near the mouth of the Seine, a fierce wind blew up, and the little girl saw her mother's terror, partly caused by the memory of the hurricane of twenty years before. The happiness of the family reunion held its own sadness, for Josephine saw the deteriorating condition of her youngest sister, who had scurvy. But there were lazy days travelling by palanquin over the island visiting 'one plantation after another', and exciting nights watching the negro dancers.

When news of unrest came from France, Josephine was anxious to be back with Eugène. Rumours of disturbances in Paris stirred up trouble on the island, where the white inhabitants were threatened with instant extermination by their slaves, and when Josephine and Hortense managed to catch the first ship that sailed for home, they had to leave virtually all their possessions behind. Holding Hortense's hand in one of hers, and a small bundle in the other, Josephine literally ran through cannon-fire to the ship.

As a mother Josephine mixed the greatest love with occasional practical fecklessness, or at least the inexperience of someone who had always had maids to look after her children. She found spots of blood on the cabin floor one day, and, examining Hortense's feet, found that they were bleeding. She

The demolition of the Bastille

Depart des Heroines de Paris pour Versailles le 5 Octobre 1789.

It was the women of Paris who marched on Versailles on 5 October 1789

Robespierre, who ruled throughout the Terror

The executioners vied with each other in committing atrocities

had been showing the sailors the negro dances she had learned in Martinique, and had worn through the soles of her shoes completely. The child burst into tears because she knew her deck excursions would now come to an end, for there were no more shoes, and Josephine, hating the thought of her daughter's disappointment at being made to spend the rest of the voyage in a cabin, burst into tears as well. The hullaballoo must have been considerable, since one of the mates, a man called Jacques, looked in to find out the cause of the tears. When Josephine explained, he promised to sew Hortense a pair of shoes himself, if Josephine would cut them out of an old pair of his own. As Empress, she looked back on this pair of shoes as the best present she had ever been given, far outweighing all the diamonds she was showing her ladies-in-waiting when she remembered the incident.

Over the next few years Josephine was to have every chance to develop her sense of true values, which had always in fact been fairly consistent: she loved glamour, but family, humanity and happiness came first.

According to Hortense, it was when they docked at Toulon on 29 October 1790 that they heard that the Revolution was a fact. She was no longer addressed as *Madame la Vicomtesse* but as *Citoyenne* (Citizeness).

The outline of the main events had already reached them abroad. The *philosophes,* who had already been expounding the evils of French society, made worse by an immense increase in population which produced a surplus of labour but a shortage of food, now found their words overtaken by the real dangers of a fierce inflation and bad harvests. In 1788 a wet spring and hail ruined another harvest. The price of bread rose to the equivalent of three-quarters of a day-labourer's wages – but many had no wages at all, and there were riots for bread. Louis XVI, roused on the July night when the Bastille fell to be told of the disturbances, had declared, astonished, 'It's a revolt.' He was gently warned by the Duke of Liancourt, Grand Master of the Wardrobe, 'No, Sire, it's a revolution.' By the autumn the royal family, who had resided at Versailles since Louis XIV deserted the capital some hundred years before, knew the meaning of hardship themselves: when a mob of Parisian women set out, armed with sticks, to walk to Versailles, they little knew that the Dauphin himself was complaining to his mother, the unpopular Austrian-born Queen, Marie-Antoinette, 'Mama, I'm so hungry'.

The King and his family agreed to return to Paris to share the famine with the people, and moved back into the old palace of the Tuileries. There was savage butchery in the streets, and some hated heads were then displayed on pikes, but the slaughter was not yet on a colossal scale, and many appear to have hoped that if it were ignored rather than exaggerated the bloodshed would cease. On 13 October 1789 the King's younger sister, Mme Elisabeth, wrote with tragic lack of prescience and sensitivity: 'All is quiet here [Paris] and I like the people much more than those of Versailles. The Court is established on the old footing. People are received every day. On Sunday, Tuesday and Thursday there is gaming. Public dinners on Sunday and Thursday . . . there is plenty of bread.'

Louis XVI was still, at this point, nominally the executive head of France. However, the old States-General, consisting of the three Estates of Nobles, Clergy, and Commons, no longer functioned: the Commons had turned themselves, by a hairs-breadth legal majority, into the ruling section of a new National Assembly. This take-over of power by the Commons had been facilitated by a few of the clergy (from Poitou) and many of the younger sons of the nobility, including Alexandre, who had joined the benches of the Third Estate and voted for the Commons' new power. Many older sons, like Alexandre's brother François, the Count of Beauharnais, remained loyal to the old system and later emigrated.

When the King tried to prevent the first meeting of the new National Assembly, by locking the chamber doors, they merely met instead on a tennis court. Alexandre's own reward for his support was immediate and striking, if not enduring. He was elected, in November 1789, one of the three secretaries to the National Assembly. In 1791 his portrait was paired with that of Robespierre, and it was Alexandre who told the House of the King's bungled attempt to flee to true safety, the 'flight to

Varennes'. He then issued the warrant for the King's arrest. At this time, there was some truth in the claim later made by his children that Alexandre was the First Gentleman of France. It was ironic that Josephine should twice be married to such men; but for the moment, though some reflected glory was shed on the family, she could not really share Alexandre's feelings. They were now, largely no doubt because of the children, on cordial and even friendly terms, but their establishments were entirely separate.

Alexandre's future downfall was indirectly helped by the Constitution of 1791. This still nominally left the King with some powers, including the right of veto; but it would allow no 'deputy' or member of the last Assembly to sit in the new one (one way to stimulate political chaos), so, debarred from political progression, Alexandre resumed his life as a soldier. There his preference for words over actions took time to show. He became a general. In April 1792 war was declared against Austria (then consisting of Hungary and Bohemia) and Prussia joined the enemies of revolutionary France; and in the late summer Alexandre was appointed chief-of-staff to the Armies of the Rhine.

In August the newly elected and very powerful left-wing Commune of Paris mobbed the Tuileries palace. The defending soldiers were overcome, the King and his family imprisoned. Sure of what was in store for him, Louis read carefully, among some 250 books during his five months in prison, the account of the execution of Charles I of England. In January 1793 he himself would go to the guillotine.

The interim saw the extreme phase of the Revolution. The moderate, idealistic Girondins were being chased from power by the extreme left, known as The Mountain. In the terrible September massacres, known supporters of the imprisoned royal family, and even such enlightened people as the Duke of Rochefoucauld, were butchered in front of their families or arrested and later executed at the rate of 1,100 per day. The scenes were such that no one who witnessed them, lost friends or relatives in them, or stood in danger themselves, could ever again expect to apply their old standards to life. Children and young people threw heads in the air and caught them on pikes. According to their guiding sentiment, people dipped handkerchiefs – or bread – in the streams of blood flowing from the victims. Corpses were sexually disfigured. There was cannibalism. The physician, surnamed 'Guillotin', who had invented the guillotine to ease death for the criminal condemned now suffered agonies of mind as it was turned into an instrument to make the mass murderers' task easy.

Nothing, and nobody, would ever be quite the same again.

For Josephine, always an easy prey to terror, the danger her children might stand in was the main concern. On the day when the Tuileries were mobbed she rushed from Paris, where she was now living off the Boulevard St Germain, to be with Hortense at her convent school of Abbaye-aux-Bois: this was soon, like the churches, to be closed by order of the anti-religious government. After the King's execution she was determined to get the children away to safety and she entrusted them both (Eugène had been sent by his father to a military school) to some good and kind friends: Prince Frederick of Salm-Kyrbourg and his sister Amelia. The Prince had originally been a friend of Alexandre's, and an ardent supporter of the revolution. Events, particularly as they affected the aristocracy, were beginning to change his mind, and he was planning to emigrate to England.

Even the children themselves, now aged eleven and nine, were not told that this was more than 'a holiday', but unfortunately Alexandre got wind of the plan. His brother had already emigrated and he must have felt that he himself was in danger of falling under suspicion. He demanded that the children should be returned from the Prince's country estate, where he was awaiting a good moment to depart. The good-natured Amelia and Frederick obeyed, and the latter paid for their return to Paris with his life.

Josephine had once told Aunt Edmée that she was 'too indolent to take sides' in the Revolution. In practical terms this was true. But while Josephine had always, as in Martinique, opposed oppression, the safety of those she loved was always her chief guide. Many of their friends had already died; her father had been a page to the guillotined Louis's mother; their very name held danger. Now that Alexandre was no longer benefiting from the early and idealistic stage of the Revolution, she had almost certainly reverted to royalist leanings. But she would always take pity on any unfortunate person, queen or beggar: in later years she once rebuked her ladies sternly for laughing at an old down-and-out trying to imitate a band for their amusement while he was starving. She was, however, shrewd enough in the ways of the world to disguise any overt sympathies for those who were mainly oppressed at the present time – until danger touched her own relations by marriage.

Alexandre's position was becoming increasingly uncomfortable, and after undue publicity was given both to his womanizing and to his absence from the battlefield in moments of battle, he was forced to resign his commission. This was accepted on the grounds that he had 'neither the strength nor the moral energy' to be a republican general.

Only one month later, in September 1793, the terrifying 'Law of Suspects' was passed by the new body, the Convention, which had in its turn superseded the National Assembly. The Convention was under the thumb of the most despotic revolutionary group yet spawned: the dreaded and sinisterly misnamed Committee of Public Safety. Under the new law people could be arrested and executed as 'a friend of tyranny and an enemy of liberty' simply, and most often, for having a title.

Josephine's sister-in-law, Françoise, the Countess of Beauharnais, had already been imprisoned, and Josephine showed that extraordinary mixture of superficial flexibility and fundamental loyalty and tenacity that were hall-marks of her character whenever she or her family was threatened. She immediately moved out of Paris to suburban Croissy, and from there in January she wrote a letter to Vadier, president of the Committee, pleading for her sister-in-law but begging him not to confuse Françoise's husband, the emigré Count, with his brother the revolutionary Alexandre. She declared: 'Mine is a republican household, and I can sign myself an out-and-out sans-culotte.' (Sans-culottes were the uniform of the revolutionaries, long tight pantaloons that were worn instead of the courtly knee-breeches.) Such a letter could only draw attention to herself and her new address, however; in spite of her pleas for Alexandre, he was arrested on his estate in March 1794, and in April Josephine herself was denounced. A search of her house at Croissy revealed mainly 'a host of patriotic letters', but she was nevertheless taken to the former Carmelite convent, now a prison, to which Alexandre had also been transferred. It was now written in his notes that he was 'accused of being suspected': 115 priests, including the archbishop of Arles, had been hacked to pieces there, and the walls and floors were still stained with their blood.

Neither Josephine nor her husband could have had much hope for their own survival. Josephine had not even had the heart to waken her children to say goodbye to them; in her absence, they were looked after by a good-hearted, slightly eccentric relation of Alexandre's, Aunt Fanny. They came frequently to the prison gates, Josephine's little pug, Fortuné, often slipping through the gates with messages under his collar.

The makeshift prisons (most of them former convents) were not equipped for such emergencies, which meant that though the overcrowding and filth were appalling, the inmates had freedom to mix and talk. Josephine at first was one of eighteen in a room, and then shared a room with three other women, including the Duchess d'Aiguillon and a girl called Delphine Custen, who was soon having an affair with Alexandre: the last of his life. Everyone made as much of a pretence as possible that life was normal. Each prisoner had half a bottle of wine a day (now cheaper than water) and abundant bread, which was more than most free men got. Cleanliness, dress and manners were still considered of great importance. A contemporary writing of another of the prisons, the Conciergerie, from which Marie-Antoinette had been taken to her death, wrote: 'As a general rule the women of the world . . . kept alive to the last word the sacred fires of good form and good taste . . . I noticed that all the women who could do so stuck to the rule of three costumes per day.' Those who had no change of clothing spent the first hour of each day washing out what they had on, and

The fashionable "victim's shirt"
The warrant for Josephine's arrest
General Hoche, who was imprisoned with Josephine

'not even the arrival of a warrant could have deterred them'.

It was absolutely not done to show fear or distress, and here, as usual, Josephine fell short of the ruthless standards of aristocratic France. To the embarrassment of her cell-mates, she wept a great deal. However, she also impressed them by her sweetness. Even Delphine was impressed by her charm, and the notorious Englishwoman of the time, Mrs Elliott, described her as 'one of the most accomplished, good-humoured, women I ever met with'. Alexandre rated the description of a 'coxcomb'.

Josephine also played solitaire (she remained a great player of games all her life) and, in her more optimistic moments, tried to tell her own future from a pack of tarot cards. She even found enough spirit to indulge in a romance of her own, with another young general, Lazare Hoche, a handsome and good-humoured man of twenty-six whom she met in the prison courtyard. According to Mrs Elliott, some prisoners were allowed a private room for important rendezvous; if this is true it may be that a room assigned to Josephine and Alexandre for their last farewell was used by them both in their 'escapist' prison love affairs. It is certainly true that Josephine and Hoche, who spent only twenty days under the same prison roof, became deeply attached to each other as a result of their affection *in extremis*.

On 23 July Alexandre was charged, under a new and still more savage law known as the 'Law of Prairial', with being an enemy of the people. The next day he was judged guilty and immediately guillotined.

General Hoche had already been transferred to the Conciergerie, presumably to await execution, and one morning the gaoler entered Josephine's cell and told her he wanted her bed. Years later Mlle Ducrest heard the Empress tell this story, and wrote it down as follows:

'Does that imply that Mme Beauharnais is to have a better one?' Mme d'Aiguillon demanded sharply.

'It means she'll not be needing one of any kind,' he replied with a repulsive grin. 'It means they're coming to take her to the Conciergerie and from there to the guillotine.'

At these words my companions emitted piercing shrieks. Finally, to put an end to their lamentations, I told them that their distress was ridiculous, that not only would I not be put to death, I would live to become a Queen of France, as had been predicted to me.

'Then why not begin making out a list of your ladies-in-waiting?' Mme d'Aiguillon inquired sarcastically.

To this Josephine replied 'I promise you the appointment' (and she would certainly have kept the promise had not Napoleon refused, with what was soon to become ironic reasoning, to have a *divorced* duchess attending the Empress).

Librairie Hachette

1363

Most of the Revolutionary Tribunals, like this one of September 1792, were composed of men who had no knowledge of the law. They sentenced all but a handful of those brought before them to death

An execution

Snark Int.

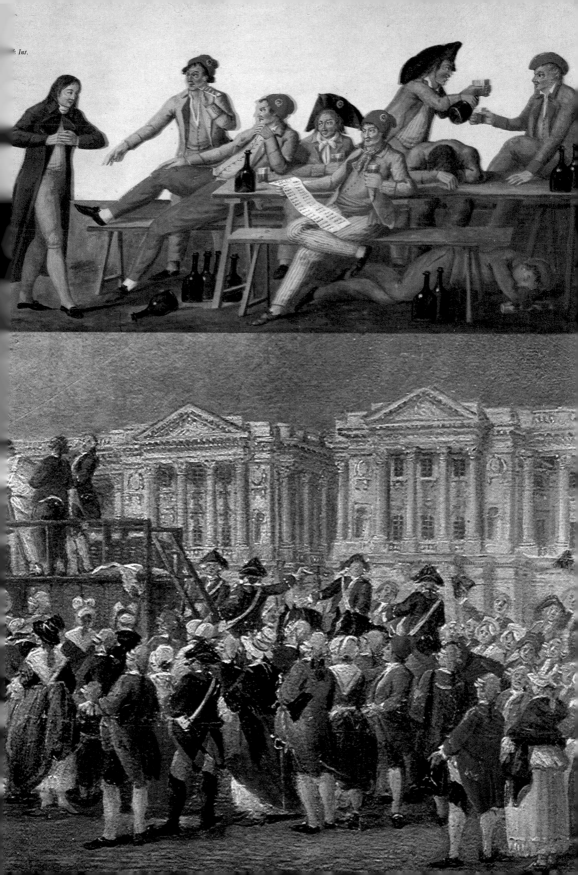

Then, thinking that the Duchess was about to faint, Josephine pulled her to the window. Outside she saw a woman enacting a strange pantomime, repeatedly pointing to her dress, and then picking up a stone. By degrees Josephine understood and called out first 'Robe?' (dress) and then 'Pierre?' (stone). The woman nodded vigorously, then went through the motions of slitting her throat. The prisoners could hardly believe that she really meant that the dictator who had authorized the extremities of the past few months was dead; but a few minutes later the charade was confirmed by a jubilant crowd. The fearful Robespierre had indeed fallen. After his arrest, the governor of the prison to which he was sent refused to receive him, and he was therefore taken to the *Hôtel de Ville* (the town hall) where, in an attempt to assassinate him, someone shot away half his jaw. A few hours later the man himself who had authorized so many deaths was guillotined.

Josephine continued: 'They brought me back my bed of leather-strip webbing, on which I slept the soundest night's sleep of my life.'

It was only three days since Alexandre had gone to the guillotine. The luck that saved Josephine was not only the timing of Robespierre's death. It was apparently helped by the extraordinary activity of a minor actor, La Bussière, who was employed by the Committee of Public Safety, and is said to have regularly chewed up and swallowed the dossiers of favourite prisoners: Josephine afterwards sent him a thousand francs. The beauty of her good friend, Thérèse de Fontenay, another unhappy young wife in the same prison who had previously taken as a lover (and would later marry) the young journalist Tallien, was another legendary factor. It was apparently after Thérèse sent her lover the news that the date for her death was approaching that Tallien instigated the attack on Robespierre.

Hortense, then aged eleven, later recalled that a 'lady of remarkable beauty' called on Eugène and herself to assure them that their mother would soon be released. This was Thérèse, then aged twenty-two; and on 6 August Josephine was freed. She was now thirty-one, and newly-widowed; and she was about to embark on the best years of her life.

Louis XVI, the last of the Condé line to sit on the throne of France. His execution started new wars in Europe

Lalance/Ziolo

3. Do You Love Him?

The week after Josephine was released from her four-month ordeal, young General Bonaparte found himself under arrest. It was a question of suspected guilt by association: his promotion had come under Robespierre's rule (and he knew the dictator's younger brother); and he had only one resounding victory behind him, when he had dislodged the Spanish–British fleet from Toulon in December 1793. However, he kept icily calm during his ten days in an Antibes prison. He wrote to his old friend (and future general) Junot, who thought he should try to escape, saying that his conscience was clear, and 'so do nothing; you will only compromise me'.

Such an open attachment to life had not always been a feature of this deep-thinking, demanding, moody young man's thoughts. His loneliness at military school in France had been followed by a period of poverty and hunger as a second lieutenant during which he sometimes wrote down reflections on suicide. He wrote to his mother that he ate 'only one meal a day', and strangers noted that he could not afford gloves, then *de rigeur*, while the daughters of his Corsican friends the Permons roused him to a fury when they laughed at the sight of his huge army boots flapping round his half-starved shanks and christened him 'Puss in Boots'. Some time later he revenged himself on one of the girls, Laure, as she remembered, by 'pinching my nose until he made me cry out' (a favourite trick, usually affectionate!) and saying 'My dear you are a clever girl but you are satirical. Correct this disposition. Remember that a woman ceases to charm whenever she makes herself feared.' It was a lesson that Josephine knew by heart.

But his meeting with Josephine was still more than a year away in the autumn of 1794, and he was yearning to give some order to his emotional life. Judging by some of his written outpourings on this subject, his inner being must have been chaotic during his adolescence and early twenties. One day he wrote, 'I regard love as injurious to society and as destructive to the individual's happiness', and on another he decided that 'Woman is indispensable to man's animal organization; but

46

MAD.ᵐᵉ BONAPARTE.

she is even more essential to the satisfaction of his sensibilities. He must identify himself with her, must pour his heart into hers. Then the two of them, fortified against unbridled lusts, will be better enabled to enjoy the charms of life. The sweetness of this union beautifies the dreams and mitigates the sorrows of life . . .' The cynic and the romantic in him ruled by turns; but on the whole, his approach was tender rather than brutal. Even the prostitute, with whom he describes a meeting in the paths of the Palais Royal in 1787 when he was eighteen, appealed to him because she looked timid, frail, and cold.

In the first four years of the Revolution, after his father's death, Napoleon had made several visits home to Corsica to see his family and to support the French cause against the Paolists, the local party who were now looking to the British for support in their fight for independence. During the night of 13 May 1793, the Paolists took Ajaccio and raided the Bonaparte mansion. Letizia, who had received a warning message from her son, took to the hills with four of her children, and walked for hours across the harsh *maquis* to a prearranged spot where Napoleon himself, together with his elder brother Joseph, managed to pick them up in a boat.

The matriarch took her children to Marseilles, and proved as resourceful in penury as her previous excessive frugality had prepared her to be. Her three daughters were promptly sent to work in a laundry. From this reversal of fortune, perhaps, can be traced the excessive greed and competitiveness that afflicted the family, turning its dynamism into spite and conflict as well as ambition and achievement.

Napoleon was already being driven by his strong Corsican sense of family to found his own. He cast around for suitable wives, and one possibility was Desirée Clary, the sister of Julie, now married to Joseph. Negotiations for her hand progressed slowly: M. Clary commented 'One Bonaparte in the family is enough'. In September 1795 Napoleon wrote to Joseph: 'if I remain here [Paris] it is not improbable that I may be seized with an unconquerable desire for marriage.' The next day he wrote again, 'I am burning to set up house . . . either an arrangement must be made with [Desirée] or the whole thing must be broken off.' At about this time Laure Permon claims that he proposed to her recently widowed mother, a charming Corsican woman, but some fourteen years his senior. Her answer was a burst of laughter which was overheard by her children in the next room. Napoleon had his revenge some months later when Mme Permon saw him chatting to the Turkish Ambassador at a party given by Talleyrand; he afterwards explained to her, 'I told him that you are of Greek extraction.'

The proposal to Mme Permon may have been due to an onrush of warmth for the family's hospitality, and her own kindness to him, a fellow Corsican, during his hungriest years; but on St Helena he remembered Desirée as 'my first love'.

In October he was still sending messages to his 'first love'; in December he sat down at seven in the morning, still drunk with love, to write his first intoxicated, unsurpassed letter to the incomparable Josephine. He had met his ideal.

With the end of the Terror a feverish excitement had seized Paris. An almost hysterical gaiety pervaded the streets. The only crime now was not to squeeze a frenzied pleasure out of every minute of every life that had been spared. Grief was hidden beneath macabre celebrations: only relatives of those who had been guillotined could get invitations to the *bals à la victime*: and then an essential part of the ladies' attire was a scarlet ribbon round the throat, as if a severed head had been stuck back on. Napoleon himself (who by August would be appalled by this 'moral abyss' and again toying with the idea of suicide) captured the less bizarre facets of the new society in a letter he wrote to Joseph in July:

Here luxury, pleasure and the arts are reviving astonishingly. Yesterday Phèdre was played at the Opera for the benefit of a retired actress; although the prices were trebled there was an immense crowd by two o'clock. Carriages and dandies are reappearing . . . Libraries and courses of history, chemistry, botany, astronomy, etc., follow one another. Everything that can delight and make life pleasant is piled on . . . The ladies are everywhere: in the theatre, out driving, in the libraries.

You see lovely creatures in the scholar's study. Here, in this one place in all the world, they are worthy to hold the reins; and the men are mad about them, think of nothing else, and live only for and through them. A woman needs six months in Paris to know what is her due and her empire.

How very different from Corsica!

Josephine had had over a year to discover her due in post-revolutionary Paris before she met Napoleon. Her prison lover, General Hoche, had taken Eugène on his staff. Josephine later recalled her son, perhaps because her affection for her lover was waning. Hoche was also now married; like all the men in Josephine's life, he complained that she did not write often enough; not even a new sixteen-year-old wife could console him for her loss.

Hortense was sent to a school that was to become famous, Mme Campan's establishment at St Germain-en-Laye, and for this and for her own expenses Josephine was forced to find funds. Alexandre's estate had been confiscated. A friend of the Taschers, a Dunkirk banker called Emmery, had been helpful in advancing money; she felt that she and the children owed their lives to the food they had thus been able to buy. For a time she was invited daily, with some other guests, to the home of a wealthy Mme Dumoulin; each guest brought her own bread, since it was so scarce, but Josephine's own circumstances were so distressed that she alone was excused the necessity.

Then suddenly, in June 1795, she was out driving in a fine carriage behind a pair of black Hungarian horses: she had written to ask the Committee of Public Safety to compensate her for those Alexandre had lost. Next, in August, she leased a charming pavilion in the rue Chantereine, which belonged to Julie Carreau, the estranged wife (still in love with him) of the great actor Talma. She had a simply furnished salon and dining-room, an ornate bedroom with mirrors and swans, the obligatory boudoir, and five servants. She also, it seems inescapable, had more than just a good friend in her new escort Paul Barras (though Napoleon himself finally judged him a homosexual), who in October (though no soldier) was made

Commander-in-Chief of the Army of the Interior, and chose Bonaparte, a professional, as his second-in-command. Barras was described by a colleague as having 'all the tastes of an opulent, extravagant, magnificent, and dissipated prince'.

He was a profiteer, and a survivor. When the Directory replaced the Convention to govern France in the autumn of 1795, Barras received fewer votes than the other four directors, yet he was the only one of the five still in power in 1799. One *sine qua non* for holding the position of a Director was a minimum age of forty, a rule that was later to prove fatal, since Napoleon could not wait so long.

Josephine became one of Barras's hostesses in Paris. She also invited him to her villa at Croissy, and succeeded in annoying one of her neighbours by having so many luxuries (the food!) and not enough of the necessities (the dishes, which she was quite prepared to borrow).

Another of Barras's hostesses was Josephine's great friend Thérèse, and the two of them were largely responsible for making a success of the new neo-Grecian fashions: gowns were light and filmy, much was bare, and only the jewellery was heavy and opaque. One evening Thérèse claimed that her whole costume did not weigh more than two six franc coins, and proceeded to prove it by stripping in front of three dozen guests and placing the wispy garments in scales held by a servant. But another friend of Josephine's, Mme Hamelin (also a Créole), found that it was a mistake to do in front of the general public what one did with one's friends: when she tried to walk from the Luxembourg to the Champs-Elysées in a 'dress' that left her bare to the waist she was jeered at and frightened.

The new fashions suited Josephine perfectly, although she never took them to such extremes. At thirty-two, with two children (who had been wet-nursed), a friend of Hortense's called Claire (later Mme de Rémusat) remembered, 'Her figure was perfect, her limbs were flexible and delicate, her movements were easy and elegant. La Fontaine's line could never have been more aptly applied than to her: "*Et la grâce, plus belle encore que la beauté.*" '

The fullest, if not necessarily the best, description of

Josephine's appearance came from Constant, Napoleon's valet:

> Never did a woman better justify the saying that the eyes are
> the mirror of the soul. Hers, of a dark blue, were nearly
> always half-closed by long, slightly arched eye-lids, fringed
> with the most beautiful lashes ever seen; and, when she
> looked thus, one felt oneself drawn to her by an irresistible
> power. The empress would have found it difficult to impart
> severity to this bewitching look, but she could, and did, when
> necessary, make it imposing . . . but what contributed more
> than all the rest to the charm of her person was the
> entrancing tone of her voice . . . one could not perhaps assert
> that the empress was a beautiful woman, but her face, so
> expressive of feeling and goodness, and the angelic grace
> which characterized her whole personality, made her the most
> attractive woman in the world.

Were her eyes really blue in some lights, although most
descriptions and paintings show them as hazel or dark?
Constant's description elsewhere of her silky, light chestnut
hair and brilliant skin is corroborated by others, but few could
look deeply into the gaze which Napoleon himself in a letter to
her called 'seductive'. What Constant and countless others
found was that Josephine had become irresistible, her mag-
netism inescapable. Her beauty was fluid, like a ballet dancer's,
and her grace was far more than physical.

Different accounts of the first meeting between Napoleon
and Josephine are probably due to some sensitivity about who
made the first move. It was, in fact, far more likely to have
been the accomplished hostess than the raw young general who
had broken too many foils when he learned fencing, rode
badly, and at about this time, according to Laure Permon (who
did not appreciate the features thought by so many others
reminiscent of a Greek or Roman coin – a product perhaps
of his distant Greek origins), was 'decidedly ugly' with his
emaciated thinness, yellow and apparently unhealthy complexion, angular features, ill-combed and ill-powdered hair, and
his usual civilian clothes of a grey great-coat, buttoned up to

his chin, a round hat which always seemed to be either over his eyes or falling off the back of his head, and a black cravat, very clumsily tied. In a word, he was unfashionable. He had, she admitted, a smile that was always agreeable; others found it as irresistible as Josephine's personality.

After yet another attempted rising in October 1795, which he put down easily, Napoleon Bonaparte, as General commanding the Army of the Interior, issued an order that all weapons should be handed in. Josephine was ready to hand over Alexandre's sword, but Eugène, when he heard this, went himself to the general's headquarters to beg to be allowed to keep it. Napoleon was touched and the sword was handed back. A few days later, according to his account, Josephine called to thank the General. Her extraordinary grace and irresistibly sweet manner fixed themselves in his mind.

Before long they met again at a dinner; she was wearing a fragile dress of Indian *mousseline de soie* with puff sleeves. It was perhaps this evening that he later remembered as the night when he fell in love: 'One day, when I was sitting next to her at table, she began to pay me all manner of compliments on my military qualities. Her praise intoxicated me. From that moment I confined my conversation to her and never left her side. I was passionately in love with her, and our friends were aware of this long before I ever dared to say a word about it.'

Her secret was so simple: she simply talked to him about what he knew best, and flattered him a little. But Josephine was seldom insincere: her ability to get on so well with others came from a natural interest in them, and an astonishingly good memory. As Mlle Ducrest wrote later, recounting the astonishment with which some visitors had heard Josephine talk about science and art: 'But Josephine could talk on any subject, and on all well . . . the Emperor used to call her his *agenda* (diary). In relating an anecdote, Napoleon would forget the date in order to give Josephine an opportunity of correcting him.'

Nevertheless, she was quite deliberate in her encouragement of the General, whose intensity and ambition made an impression on her as they did on others. On 28 October she wrote him a letter similar to letters she had sometimes written to Barras: 'You no longer come to see a friend who is fond of you. You have completely deserted her. You are wrong, for she is affectionately attached to you. Come to lunch with me tomorrow. I need to see you, and to talk with you about your affairs. Good night my friend. *Je vous embrasse.*' How faultlessly she plucked the strings. After a lunch or two with Josephine and some of her friends, the Marquis de Caulaincourt and General de Ségur, Napoleon had no desire to spend any time with anyone else. He would soon be writing 'men bore me'. The famous letter written at seven in the morning shows that physically the affair progressed satisfactorily.

On 21 January 1796, Barras gave a dinner to celebrate the third anniversary of the execution of Louis XVI. Hortense, who was thirteen, was invited, and sat between her mother and Bonaparte at the Luxembourg Palace. The evening made a great impression on her. 'In order to speak to her, he constantly thrust himself forward with such force that he tired me out and made me draw back. He spoke with fire and was solely preoccupied with my mother.' Not surprisingly, Hortense disliked this rough man, and was frightened by his attentions to her mother: supposing he should take her away from herself and Eugène? If so, 'Mama won't love us as much', she told her brother. Yet although Josephine's children were slow to respond to the ardent stranger, twenty years hence they would be showing him the greatest loyalty and affection possible. And even on this first night, Hortense was struck by Napoleon's appearance: in spite of herself, she had to admit that 'his face was handsome and highly expressive, although marked with an extraordinary pallor'.

Bonaparte had wanted to marry even before he met Josephine; now everything had combined. In the past he had planned marriages – and averted them – for his family and friends, so he was well aware of the social advantages of this match. 'On the whole,' he said at St Helena, 'the marriage was an excellent thing for me. A good French family suited me very well, as I was Corsican by birth.' However, he was not as calculating about his own potential wives as he was about other people's, as his proposal to Mme Permon had already shown. And now he was quite madly in love, to the point where he really did sometimes fear for his own reason. He must *possess* Josephine; he thought he might achieve this by marrying her.

It was very different for Josephine, who was intrigued and impressed, but not at all infatuated, with her lover. This strange man, whose passion, intensity of ambition and penetration of thought seemed still odder against her own bland background and the sophistication of the Paris salons, half-amused, half-confused her. Her instinctive reaction was perhaps not so different from that of a dog which barks when it sees a strangely dressed man, or that of another young woman who said she would not like to meet Napoleon alone in a wood at night. To the poet Antoine-Vincent Arnault she expressed it in that charming Créole accent and four words he would never forget: 'Il est *drolle*, Bonaparte.'

Her first reaction to his proposal seems to have been one of surprise, and negation. Surely he could not think that because she was his mistress she was willing to become his wife! Why couldn't they go on just as they were? He had qualities that attracted her, but not the attributes that would make him an irresistible suitor. She also had to cope with Hortense, who each time she came to Paris from school pleaded with her: 'I cried and begged her not to re-marry, but her reassurances to me became less and less convincing.'

Josephine was able to be extraordinarily honest about her own feelings (if not those of her children, whom she portrayed as orphans urging her to provide them with a new father – perhaps a projection of one of her own thoughts about the proposal) when she wrote to a friend at this time:

'Do you love him?' is naturally your first question.
My answer is perhaps – No.
'Do you dislike him?'
No again – but the feelings I have for him are of that lukewarm kind which true devotees think worst in all matters of religion. Now, love being a sort of religion, my feelings ought to be very different from what they really are. This is the point on which I want your advice ... to come to a

decision has always been too much for my Créole inertness, and I find it easier to obey the wishes of others.

I admire the General's courage; the extent of his information on every subject on which he converses; his shrewd intelligence, which enables him to understand the thoughts of others before they are expressed; but I confess I am somewhat fearful of that control which he seems anxious to exercise on all about him. There is something in his penetrating gaze that cannot be described . . . He talks of his passionate love for me with a seriousness that makes it impossible to doubt his sincerity, yet this . . . is precisely what has stopped me from giving the consent which I have often been on the point of giving . . .

My spring of life is past. Can I then hope to preserve for any length of time this ardent love which in the General amounts almost to madness? If his love should cool, as it certainly will, after our marriage, will he not reproach me for having prevented him from making a better match? . . .

Barras assures me that if I marry the General he will get him appointed Commander-in-Chief of the army of Italy . . . The General said 'Do they think I cannot get forward without their patronage? One of these days they will be all too happy if I grant them mine. I have a good sword by my side which will carry me on.' What do you think of this self-confidence? Does it not savour of excessive vanity? A General to talk of patronizing the chiefs of Government? It is very ridiculous. Yet I know not how it happens, his ambitious spirit sometimes impresses me so much that I am almost tempted to believe in the practicability of any project he takes into his head – and who can foresee what he may attempt? . . .

This letter reveals the extraordinary psychological sensitivity that Josephine had developed, and that would remain the foundation of much of her goodness of heart, as well as her charm, for the rest of her life. How clearly she spelt out the possibility of her own doom, even though she could not quite foresee that in fact Bonaparte would always love her, if not as madly as at the moment. How right she was to be almost afraid of his violent passion for her, which frightened him as well. How accurately she foretold the growing obsession with power, the imagination which knew no limits and thus brought its own limitations to Napoleon himself. It is interesting that she should accuse herself of not loving him: she, who had already been through an arranged marriage, some affairs, and at least one love affair, evidently remained a romantic.

Her own experience drove her in two opposing directions. At thirty-two she was no longer considered young, and she had her future security, as well as that of her children, to consider. But her witness of her mother's unhappy marriage, and her cruel experience of her own, left her in dread.

The hint of her answer lay in the reference to her Créole indolence, and in her dependence upon the decision of others. She did not rely entirely upon others, but she was certainly a very feminine and dependent woman in comparison with many women bred in Paris who had keen minds and forceful personalities. Perhaps also, as a woman who had no chance to make anything of her own life separately, she was drawn all the more powerfully to someone whose obvious ambition and drive must carve a decisive life for them both.

She did not love him, perhaps partly out of self-defence, but she decided to marry him. 'My mother's resistance ended when she saw General Bonaparte on the verge of leaving,' explained Hortense. 'It fell to Mme Campan to break the news to Eugène and me; our mother lacked the courage.'

Josephine's lawyer, Ragideau, was horrified by the news, and tried to dissuade her from tying herself to a younger man with nothing except 'his cape and his sword'. Napoleon, who had overheard this conversation, promptly awarded the lawyer a vote of confidence for his honesty, and asked him to act for both of them in future! (He was later named on the imperial civil list.)

In mid-February the two had a violent quarrel, apparently caused by Josephine's doubts about the marriage and about Napoleon's motives in wanting to marry her. He had in fact checked with the banker Emmery on her property in Martinique, but this was rather a point in his favour, since her prospects did not amount to very much.

1441
an IV.   n° 290.

9 mars 1796

RÉPUBLIQUE FRANÇAISE.
LIBERTÉ, ÉGALITÉ, FRATERNITÉ.

Préfecture du Département de la Seine.

Buonaparte et de Tascher   EXTRAIT du Registre des Actes de Mariage
. de *L'an IV*

2e Mairie

DÉLIVRÉ EXTRAIT

Du dix neuvième jour du mois de Ventôse de l'an quatrième de la République.

Acte de Mariage de Napolione Bonapart, général en chef de l'armée de l'intérieur, âgé de Vingt huit ans, né à ajaciu département de la Corse, domicilié à Paris rue d'Antin, fils de Charles Bonaparte, rentier et de Letizia Ramolini /

Et de Marie Joseph Rose Detascher, âgée de Vingt huit ans, née à Lisle Martinique sous les Isles du Vent, domiciliée à Paris rue Chantereine fille de Joseph Gaspard Detascher, Capitaine de dragons, et de Rose Claire Desvergers Detanois.

devant moi Charles Théodore françois Le Clercq, officier public de l'état civil du douzième arrondissement, Canton de Paris, après avoir fait lecture en présence des parties et témoins, 1° de l'acte de naissance de Napolione Bonaparte, qui Constate qu'il est né le Cinq février mil sept Cent soixante huit de

Josephine's past does not seem to have caused the anxiety it might have been expected to in a Corsican. Although he was by nature jealous, and although he certainly knew of her past lovers, he seems to have accepted their existence with a philosophical equanimity. Barras was now keen to arrange Josephine's marriage, which partly explains Napoleon's suspicion that he was homosexual – he could not imagine any normal man finding her less than irresistible. He showed more antipathy to Hoche, and told his fortune (which was unfortunately to come true) 'General, you will dic in your bed.' But perhaps the fascination she had for others was part of her attraction for him, and he seems to have found her experience equally heady. Later he wrote 'For me, virtue was whatever you made it', and also 'More naïve and younger, I might have loved you less.'

On 8 March 1796 the marriage contract was signed. None of Bonaparte's family knew that he was to be married. Josephine, who was thirty-two, called herself twenty-eight; Napoleon, twenty-six, also called himself twenty-eight. The next day the civil marriage ceremony was performed, and the eager groom managed to be two hours late. The former Viscountess of Beauharnais, *née* Marie-Josèphe-Rose Tascher de la Pagerie, was now Mme Bonaparte: and from now on everyone would follow Napoleon in calling her 'Josephine'.

He had apparently won her; but as yet the victory was small. Josephine, tenacious as ever in her loyalty, refused that night to allow Fortuné, the dog which had carried messages to her in prison, to be put off the bed by her new husband. He later told the writer Arnault: 'I was told that I had the choice of sleeping in another bed or sharing that one with Fortuné. The situation rather annoyed me, but it was a question of take it or leave it. So I resigned myself. The favourite was less accommodating than I – of which I bear proof on this leg.'

How unlike the girl of sixteen who had married the Viscount exactly half a lifetime ago. And the passionate young general, who thought that after all his youthful sufferings he was about to possess all he wanted for the moment in this world, the woman and the command, was to suffer all the torments of love for which his intensity of spirit had perfectly prepared him.

4. "Men Bore Me"

Napoleon's fundamental need was to understand and to be in command of any situation. This was obvious in his social life, but it also ran deep through his social and emotional needs. Better by far to be the richest man in a provincial town, he believed, than poor in Paris. He even wanted, consciously, to be in charge of death: in an early note (dated 1786) he asked himself 'Since I must die, is it not best to kill oneself?' At twenty-three, he seemed to his younger brother Lucien to 'have a strong inclination to be a tyrant', though to some extent he checked this tendency, at home if not in his foreign policy.

He believed that he wanted to dominate women as well, but perhaps this was really only true on the intellectual plane, on which he could be downright contrary with them. He once said, 'If a woman were to advocate some political move, that would seem to me sufficient reason for taking the opposite course.'

In Josephine he had chosen a woman who, while extraordinarily feminine, was an emotional challenge to him. She had not been over-eager to marry him, but had been persuaded; then, on his wedding night, he had discovered that she was not willing to comply with any wish of her bridegroom that would involve discomfort for her dog. He soon found that, at a much deeper level, this often insecure, dependent, fragile, volatile woman still retained a sense of complete independence of himself, her husband. Perhaps this was the challenge he needed to unleash all the mixed feelings in his tremendously variable personality; at any rate the challenge was overwhelming, and turned his already passionate love into corrosive burning agony. The future Emperor and Empress had the briefest and most modest of honeymoons in her little house before this facet of their relationship fully revealed itself. On 10 March the day after the wedding, they visited Josephine's children at their schools. Napoleon teased Hortense, trying to gain her confidence, but alienated her still further. With a bluntness and courage that matched his own, the thirteen-year-old girl soon wrote to ask him why, when he had such a low opinion of women, he had married one of them. ·

Napoleon's earth-shaking victory at the Arcola Bridge in 1796 was commemorated by Gros

Snark Int.

" The heroine of Peschiera" – Josephine's second taste of gunfire : her coach was fired
on by an Austrian gun-boat on Lake Garda

Snark Int.

Snark Int.

Librairie Hachette

The fashionable walk past the
Palais Royal

Directory society decreed new
fashions for men

Clothes and even hairstyles were
frankly erotic compared with the
elaborate pre-revolutionary
styles – like the one of 1780

A mania for dancing was part of
the post-Terror reaction

Batsford

*Thérèse Tallien, Josephine's friend
and another of Barras's mistresses,
was one of the most fashionably
beautiful women*

*Paul Barras was one of the five
Directors elected in September 1795*

The French enter Milan in 1795

Then the day after that, on 11 March, General Bonaparte left the pavilion in the rue Chantereine to take command of the Army of Italy. The honeymoon had lasted thirty-six hours.

To France's traditional enemies, Austria and Prussia, had now been added, following the regicide, England, Holland, and Spain.

The Army of Italy was in a sad state. Although its record was good – Nice and Savoy had long been taken by the French, who now held the Italian coast as far as Savona – many supplies had been cut off by the English, who were blockading the coast. Some of the North Italian states who had previously shown some sympathy to France had also been appalled by the murder of Louis XVI and by the new atheist regime, and were turning instead to the Allies. Now the Army had to face the Austrians, the Sardinians, and the Piedmontese.

Not only ladies found Napoleon lacking in poise at this time: even his A.D.C. Antoine Marmont noted that he was awkward and undignified, but also that as soon as he spoke to the troops he was impressive. Another witness simply said that as soon as he put on his General's hat he was two feet taller. His psychology in addressing the Army at Nice was simple: 'Soldiers! You are naked and ill-fed; the Government owes you a great deal and can give you nothing ... I will lead you into the most fertile plains in the world ... you will find there honour, glory and fortune. Soldiers of the Army of Italy, will you be lacking in courage and constancy?' And it was effective, for it was based on his own young aspirations.

Napoleon had once looked back upon the ideal life enjoyed by former heroic Corsicans. 'Proud and filled with a noble sense of his personal importance, a Corsican was happy if he had spent the day in public affairs. The night passed in the tender arms of a beloved wife ... Love and nature made his nights like those of the gods.' He had had two such nights. Then, as he travelled along the road to Genoa, he felt the first twinges of the tug-of-war between love and ambition. A stream of letters flowed from his heels back to Paris. On 30 March 1796 he wrote:

Not one day passes without my loving you. Not one night passes without my holding you in my arms. I have not drunk a cup of tea without cursing the glory and ambition that keep me far from the soul of my life...If, in the middle of the night, I get up to work, it is only because that may advance by a few days the arrival of my sweet friend...I ask of you neither eternal love nor fidelity, but only truth, complete honesty. The day upon which you said 'I love you less' would be the last day of my love – or the last of my life...Nature forged my soul strong and resolute, she wove yours out of gossamer and lace...oh, if you love me less, it can only be that you have never loved me. Then I should indeed be an object of pity.

On 3 April he wrote:

I have received all your letters, but none has made such an impression on me as the last...what style! What feelings you show! They are fire and they burn my poor heart...

To live for Josephine, that is the story of my life...Oh my adorable wife! I don't know what fate has in store for me, but if it keeps me apart from you any longer, it will be unbearable. My courage will not be enough for that...the thought that my Josephine may be in trouble, that she may be ill, above all the cruel, the terrible thought that she may love me less sinks my heart, slows my blood...to die not loved by you, to die without knowing, would be the torment of hell...

Men bore me. I ought to hate them. They take me away from my heart...forgive me, sweetheart, I am raving; Nature is frail when one feels deeply, when one is loved by you.

Bonaparte.
Sincere friendship to Barras, Sucy, Mme Tallien; respects to Mme Chateau-Renard; true love to Eugène, to Hortense.

Goodbye, goodbye! I shall go to bed without you, sleep without you. Let me sleep, I beg you. For several nights I have felt you in my arms; a happy dream, but it is not you.

On 7 April:

I am displeased. Your letter is as cold as friendship . . . but what inconsistency on my part! I complained that your last letter wrought havoc in my soul, disturbed my sleep, aroused my senses. I said I wanted colder letters. But they bring me the chill of death . . . A kiss below your breast, and lower – still lower.

On 24 April:

You let many days go by without writing to me. What then are you doing? No, my love, I am not jealous, but sometimes anxious. Come quickly, now, to join me. I warn you, if you delay longer you will find me ill . . .

Junot is bringing 22 flags to Paris. You are to come back with him, do you understand? He is not to return without you . . .

But travel carefully . . . what if you had an accident, fell ill, or felt exhausted – come carefully, my love, but think of me often.

I have received a letter from Hortense. I will write to her. She is altogether charming. I love her and will soon send her the perfumes she wants.

Read [Ossian's] poem *Carthon* carefully . . .

A kiss on your heart, and one lower down, much lower!

B.

I don't know if you need money; you have never talked to me about your affairs.

If so, you can go to my brother, who has 200 louis belonging to me.

On 29 April:

Today I beg you to travel with Murat instead, to come via

68

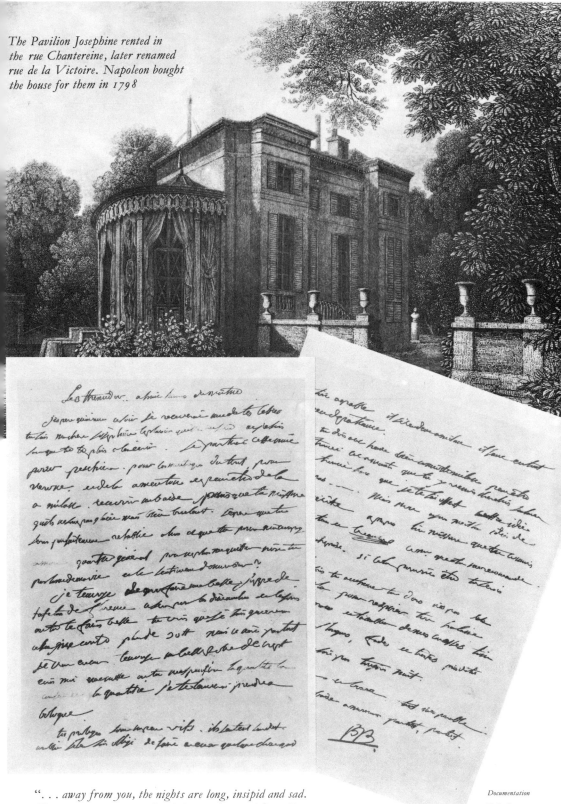

The Pavilion Josephine rented in the rue Chantereine, later renamed rue de la Victoire. Napoleon bought the house for them in 1798

"... away from you, the nights are long, insipid and sad. Close to you one regrets that it is not always night..."
letter from Napoleon to Josephine, 21 July 1796

Documentation

Tallandier

Turin. That will cut your travelling by two weeks. So I may see you here within 15 days...

Never was a woman loved with greater tenderness, fire or devotion. Never has a woman been in such complete mastery of another's heart... If it is different for you... then my soul, maimed for life, would never again wholly trust itself to respond to any emotion of tenderness or ecstasy. Then I would live solely on the physical plane...

No letters from you. I only get one every four days; instead, if you loved me, you would write twice a day.

But you must chatter with the little gentlemen visitors from ten o'clock in the morning, and then listen to all the stupidities and gossip of a hundred young whipper-snappers until one in the morning.

In countries which have some morals, everyone is at home by ten o'clock at night. But in those countries one writes to one's husband, one thinks about him, one lives for him.

Goodbye Josephine, for me you are a monster which I cannot explain.

A kiss on your mouth, or on your heart. There is no-one but me, is there? And then, one on your breast.

How lucky Murat is – [that] little hand.

B.

One wonders whether Napoleon, who had nineteen horses killed under him in battles throughout his life, ever showed more courage than in laying himself so completely bare in his love life. He admitted his complete subservience to Josephine. But the affectionate asides about her children and what she should read, his sudden concern with the practicalities of money and travelling, all show the basic resilience of this many-sided man. For the moment he did not, except at moments of doubt, resent the thrall in which she held him, because he believed himself loved in return. It speaks loudly of Josephine's loving and beguiling ways when they were together.

But Josephine did not come; did not want to come. She could write once every four days, which was probably quite

70

a lot for her; she could express feelings that set his senses on fire again; but she could not love him, and still more she could not want to leave Paris to be with him.

Since she was eventually to love him at least as devotedly as he did her – with less passion but greater single-mindedness – why did she not love him now? Partly no doubt because the element of madness in his passion frightened her, a fact he later realized, and perhaps also because she was frightened to believe in his love too much in case it changed. But such devotion was balm to a heart that had been spurned in her first marriage, and, with an immaturity that could touch some and shock others, she showed the letters to anyone who was interested to know how madly she was loved this time.

Away from him, she was having a marvellous time in Paris. She was always a pleasure-loving and sociable woman who loved the company of her friends and got a good deal of fun out of parties: now still more invitations to the salons arrived with each of Bonaparte's astonishing successes. These were remarkable not only because the section of the army he was commanding was considered more or less a rabble, but also for the speed with which he routed in turn the Piedmontese, the Sardinians, and the Austrians, and the unusual, lightning thrusts with which he scored each victory. Josephine was also busy, planning the new decor of her house (in a military style very flattering to her new husband), and still trying to console her children for her re-marriage.

Even the Directory did not want her to join Napoleon: General Carnot, a member of the Directory, feared that more love might mean fewer victories. So his private and almost stoically phrased plea to Barras, 'I very much wish for my wife to join me', brought no success. It was agreed that she should not be allowed to set out until Milan had been taken.

On his way south, Bonaparte had stopped in Marseilles to inform his mother and the rest of the family about his marriage. Letizia had been widowed when Napoleon was seventeen, and though he was her second son he was already beginning to look, as he had long behaved, like the head of the family. Letizia, and still more her daughters, were born with iron in their soul, and a clannish Corsican contempt for outsiders. The news of his marriage to a fashionable but poor Parisian widow (and no doubt the sight of his evident infatuation) must have rung in the family's heart like a knell, judging by the cold letters Josephine soon received from Letizia and from Joseph.

The spear-head of the Bonapartes' attack on Josephine as the years passed was to be her failure to give Napoleon children. It was unfortunate – and perhaps owed more to her memory that even Alexandre had been less demanding when she was pregnant than to any real belief that she was pregnant – that she now raised false hopes in a man to whom family was of such supreme importance. Napoleon received the news in a letter from Murat, and wrote one of the most charming, generous, and tender of even his extraordinary love letters to her (it was written three days after his victory at the Battle of Lodi, a moment which he would later look back upon as crucially decisive in terms of his sense of destiny).

13 May, 1796

So it is true that you are pregnant. Murat has written to me, but he tells me that it is making you ill and that he thinks it unwise for you to undertake so long a journey. So I must still be deprived of the joy of holding you in my arms! I must still spend several months far from all that I love! Is it possible that I shan't have the pleasure of seeing you with your little belly? That should make you interesting indeed... Your letter is short and sad and shakily written. What is it, my adorable one? What can be upsetting you? Oh! Don't stay in the country; go to town, try to amuse yourself, and remember that there is no truer torment for my soul than to know that you are unwell and unhappy. I thought I was jealous, but I swear to you that I am not. I think I would rather give you a lover myself than know you were miserable...

As Marmont, one of Bonaparte's aides and later a Marshal of France said, 'Bonaparte was in love in the full sense of the phrase, in all its force and in its widest meaning. It was, to judge by appearances, his first passion, and he experienced it with the full vigour of his nature... Although she no longer had the freshness of youth she knew how to please him, and we know that to lovers the question 'why' is superfluous. One loves because one loves, and nothing is less susceptible to explanation and analysis than this emotion.'

Certainly the mixture of the carnal, the tender, the demanding and the protective in Napoleon's letters show that at this time love was expanding his nature and bringing out, as well as occasional feelings of jealousy, some of his greatest qualities of generosity and imagination.

Yet if Josephine's possible pregnancy left her feeling too weak to undertake a long and difficult journey over appalling roads, it did not prevent her from making the rounds she enjoyed in Paris. During the week when Murat's letter was written, she and Thérèse Tallien were seen everywhere together, escorted by Murat. She also took Thérèse with her to watch the victory celebrations at the Luxembourg, and when Junot, who presented the captured standards, escorted them down the Palace stairs, the crowd called out cheering her and naming her 'Notre-Dame-des-Victoires' (Our Lady of Victory). There was more than a little in it, and Josephine, who knew that Napoleon was almost as superstitious about his 'lucky star' as she herself was about fortune tellers, nurtured the idea.

On 21 May, Carnot wrote telling Napoleon that she had been given permission to leave Paris: 'It is with great reluctance that we yield to the desire of the Citizenness Bonaparte to join you. We were afraid that the attention you would give her would turn you from the attention due to the glory and safety of your country . . . we have agreed with her that she could set out only when Milan was yours. You are there, and we have no more objections to make.'

It was in fact more than a month before Josephine made use of the Directory's permission and left for Milan. This hardly sounds like the speed of a woman who had been pleading to join her husband. It seems that in spite of all his letters, Napoleon had failed to keep alive the spark of interest she had felt in him when they married. As well as being immature and rather shallow, if not deliberately callous, at this time in her life, Josephine lacked imagination enough to remind her of what Napoleon was like now that he was away (though just married, they had known each other for six months, and well for three, before he left). She did not love him and she was selfish enough to make this obvious, though she bore his name and, just possibly, his child. Hers was not a positive cruelty, such as Alexandre had shown to her, but a negative carelessness the more obvious because she was, in the actual presence of distress or pain, unusually kind-hearted. She stopped writing.

Napoleon read the signs, and on 11 June he wrote:

> ...where will this letter reach you? If in Paris, then my despair is certain – then you no longer love me, and all that is left for me is to die...
>
> I hate women, Paris, love. I am in a dreadful state and your conduct – But should I reproach you? No. Your conduct is decreed by your destiny.
>
> Embrace your lovely children for me. Since I must no longer love you, I love them the more. Despite fate and honour, I shall love you all my life.

In his next letter, of 14 June, he showed great insight, as well as the remorse of the lover who fears he may have harmed his own cause, or, worse, caused actual harm to the beloved:

> ...perhaps I wrote to you in terms too violent. If my letters have wounded you, I shall be inconsolable for life...I must know first of all that you forgive the mad, frenzied letters I have written you. If you are well enough to reason, you will realize that the overwhelming love that fills me has perhaps unbalanced my mind...
>
> Murat tries to convince me that your illness is not grave – but you do not write to me. It is more than a month since I had a letter from you.

He wrote to Joseph, the brother he still loved, begging for

news: 'you know...that Josephine is the first woman I have loved. Her illness causes me to despair.'

For a man with a mind as analytical and incisive as Napoleon's, the uncertain nature of Josephine's complaint, and still more the elusive nature of the loved one herself, created a double torment of questioning. Count Bertrand later described the thing that characterized his mind as 'his ability to focus his attention on a single idea, to examine it from every angle, abandoning it only after he had exhausted the subject and when – according to his own typical expression – he has "grasped it, the seat, and hands and feet, and by the head"...it is not unusual for him to spend ten or twelve hours on a single idea.' The effect of such intensity of thought when applied to Josephine was almost always to fall short of his love for her: admittedly, as time passed, she would add many strong qualities to her basic sweetness and sensitivity, but the essence of her, and of their passion, eluded reasoning. For the present, his brooding could only bring more doubts.

Life had become, as he said himself, a perpetual nightmare for him. His mind oscillated between images of the child that would soon be in her arms, and of a lover who might be there now. If there were one, he now wrote, he would tear his heart out and then – no, he would not harm Josephine, but would die himself. He imagined that he could no longer plan battles, though there was no evidence for this, and his triumphant letters to the Directory about victory in Lombardy and the taking of Mantua, as well as dozens of practical reports, show that he was able to retain an air of extraordinary confidence and efficiency under this terrible stress. But Marmont saw him close to: 'His wife's perpetual delaying of her departure tormented him horribly, and he began to show symptoms of jealousy and of the superstition which was a marked trait of his character. One morning...the glass of his wife's portrait shattered in his hands. His face turned so white that it frightened me, and his reaction was painful to see: "Marmont," he told me, "my wife is either ill or unfaithful."'

In mid-April (1796) Josephine had indeed met the young man who seems for a time to have excluded Napoleon from her heart.

Photo Bulloz

Murat, who married Caroline Bonaparte, and was made King of Naples by Napoleon. The couple's treachery hurt Napoleon deeply

Talleyrand, who helped to make and later to break Napoleon

Photo Bulloz

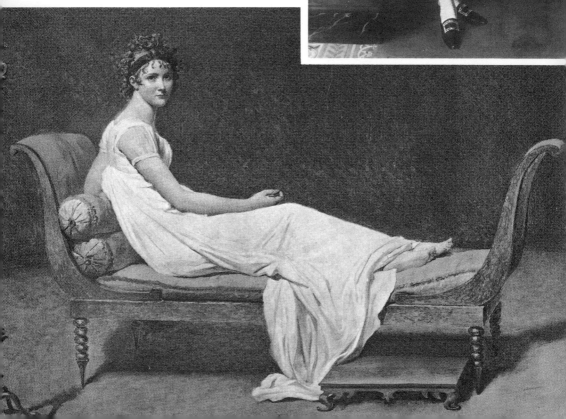

He was nine years younger than she, and in a curious, though far less malicious, way, their relationship echoed the old triangle between Josephine, Alexandre, and Laure: but Napoleon was not such an easy victim as his wife had once been.

Josephine always whole-heartedly enjoyed the company and attentions of men, and plainly when her husband left for Italy had no intention of repeating her former miserable existence as a soldier's deserted wife sitting at home. She was not in love with Napoleon, and may have felt she owed him nothing more in the way of loyalty than she had already given him by agreeing to marry him. No one knew if or when he might return, and geography lent its own force to her feeling of freedom.

Lieutenant Hippolyte Charles was twenty-four, and charming. The playwright Arnault considered him 'a delightful companion', with 'the gayest, most even disposition' – how different from the moody Bonaparte. Women found him 'dashing' in his hussar's uniform, and they too responded to his liveliness. Laure Permon declared that it was 'impossible to find a ... more amusing fellow'. Physically, she noted, he was 'small, well-made, with good features, a dark clear complexion, and hair black as jet; he was altogether attractive, though a little deficient in the polish of elegant society'. Thus in stature and in lacking the ultimate *directoire* polish, as well as in being considerably younger than herself, he resembled Napoleon. Nor were his charms limited to the superficial. He became a great friend of Laure's future husband, Junot, and the couple found him noble-hearted – a judgment borne out by the fact that unlike the many who boasted of real or desired liaisons with Josephine, he said not a word about it, and intended that all their correspondence should be burned when he died. A few letters were misplaced and survive. In his regiment they had nicknamed him 'Wide-Awake Charles'. Josephine's own enthusiasm about him shone clearly through a note she wrote to Talleyrand about a month after she had met Charles: 'You will be mad about him. Mesdames Récamier, Tallien and Hamelin have all lost their heads over him, he is so handsome. And such taste! ... I am convinced that no man had ever known before how to tie a cravat.' She also told Talleyrand, with astonishing naïveté, 'you will hear him talk and he will give you ideas'.

By June there were no further hopes for a baby for Napoleon: at one time, three doctors had been summoned to see Josephine, but whether they were there as the result of a miscarriage, or whether they were simply part of an alibi for her delay, it is impossible to judge.

The last week in June finally saw Josephine's departure from Paris.

The Directory wrote to inform Bonaparte that his wife was setting out to join him, and issued passports to her, to her maid Louise Compoint, who was to play her own part in Josephine's future difficulties, to Joseph Bonaparte and Junot, to a financier Hamelin, and to 'Citizen Hippolyte Charles, assistant to Adjutant General Leclerc of the Army of Italy'.

Paul Barras gave a farewell dinner for Josephine at the Luxembourg. There could be no turning back now, and Arnault remembers: 'Her distress was acute when she realized that she had exhausted her last excuse ... she would gladly have forgone ... all the palaces in the world for the sake of her little house in the rue Chantereine.'

After dinner, Barras himself escorted Josephine to the carriage in the courtyard, and helped her in. Arnault recalls: 'She sobbed as if she were going to the torture chamber, whereas she was going to Italy to reign as sovereign.'

Since Hippolyte Charles was to travel with her in the very same carriage, it was obviously not him Josephine was regretting: it was Paris, and her life of pleasure, the first full taste of which had only just begun to burst upon her palate after the years of hope in Martinique, the desert years with Alexandre, the agony of mind awaiting the guillotine. She was to leave her beloved home, her children and her *life* to travel to a husband she could scarcely remember, who had himself hinted to her that his mind was becoming unhinged with love.

Hamelin noted on the journey that Hippolyte Charles became sulky whenever one of the other men was enjoying Josephine's attention: this suggests not the confident lover, but the smitten lieutenant still not quite daring to hope that his charms will succeed. The point at which they did succeed remains in doubt, but it was this journey itself that was to be cited to Bonaparte, and that was to threaten his happiness and his marriage.

On 26 June, the very day that Josephine set out for Milan, Napoleon wrote to her. Though he probably only half-believed his own accusations, he in fact sketched an extremely accurate picture of her inner and outer life at this period, when she was in full social and sexual bloom:

> You were supposed to have left on the fifth Prairial [30 May by the new revolutionary calendar]; fool that I was, I expected you on the 13th. As if a pretty woman could abandon her way of life, her friends, her Mme Tallien, a dinner with Barras, a first-night at the theatre, her Fortuné – yes, Fortuné! You love everything more than you do your husband; for him you have only a little esteem, only a part of the general good-will with which your heart is filled.

Even so, he sent her kisses *everywhere* again and warned her that he would be temporarily absent from Milan when she arrived, since there were affairs to deal with at Leghorn. But since the letter crossed her own journey, she arrived expecting to find her husband. Perhaps it was as well that she had three days to rest after the journey, which had taken more than two weeks, through beautiful countryside, but over appalling roads.

Their reunion in the Serbelloni Palace lasted only a few hours longer than their honeymoon. Napoleon arrived back in Milan on 13 July, and was away again at the battle front on 15 July. But it was long enough, though even this forty-eight hours leave had to be interrupted by hours spent at his desk, planning new campaigns on old maps. Hamelin, who was keeping Josephine company for much of the time, remembers how Napoleon would burst in, and without a word to him, rush over to his wife: he 'played with her like a child, teasing her, making her cry, and covering her with bold and hearty caresses that sent me over to the window to pretend to inspect the weather'.

The effect on his spirits was wonderful and visible. Marmont recorded it: 'Once reunited with his wife at Milan, General Bonaparte was supremely happy, for he lived then only for her.

And so it was for a long time; a love so true, so pure, so exclusive, had never possessed the heart of a man, and that of a man of so superior a nature.'

As with their first night together, this further experience of passion served not to assuage, but to augment, his feelings. The night that he returned to the front line he wrote:

> A few days ago I thought I loved you, but now, since seeing you again, I love you a thousand times more. Every day since I met you I have loved you more – just to disprove La Bruyère's maxim that love comes all at once.
>
> I beg you, let me see that you have faults. Be less beautiful, less gracious, less tender, above all, less good; above all, never be jealous, never weep. Your tears rob me of my reason . . .

So one perceives that between the love-making and the public appearance at a La Scala gala performance (on 14 July, seven years after the Bastille had fallen) and his public teasing of her there had been tears and questions and explanations, and that it was not Napoleon alone who had made a show of jealousy.

Two days later the courier told him that Josephine had not written: he reproached her for being a wicked, ugly, cruel tyrant – and admitted, while asking her pardon, that he had opened two letters addressed to her! He added, 'I should like you to give me complete permission to read your letters', just as Josephine, at seventeen, had wanted to read Alexandre's.

While he was sleeping in his famous little camp bed in the Alps, waiting for the Austrians to move, Josephine was preparing to leave Milan for their next meeting at Cassano. For her, there was no promise of glory to compensate her for her physical and mental discomfort. On 23 July she wrote to Thérèse Tallien:

> The journey here was the hardest and most uncomfortable imaginable. I was on the road for eighteen days, and had a fever and a pain in my side when I got into the coach. The fever has gone but the pain remains. I am bored to death here.

Photo Bulloz

Napoleon's camp bed travelled wherever he went: even, eventually, to St Helena

In the middle of all the superb celebrations given in my honour I long all the time for my friends at Chaillot and my friends at the Luxembourg [the Talliens and Barras]. My husband doesn't love me – he worships me! I am afraid he will go mad with love. I have only seen him for a moment; he is involved with the siege of Mantua.

To her Aunt Edmée – who had finally married the Marquis, just before Josephine's departure for Italy, having at last been enabled to do so by the death of her separated husband – Josephine wrote in similar tones of her boredom with all the grandeurs heaped on her by the princes of Italy: 'well, I would rather be an ordinary individual in France. I don't like the honours of this country and am often bored.' However, she did not keep up her sophisticated and off-hand comments on her husband when it came to confiding in the family: 'I have the best husband in the world. I never need anything, for he always anticipates my wishes...he couldn't possibly be a better

81

husband...he often writes to my children for he loves them very much.'

While she could still not get the measure of her husband as a military man and as a thinker – even after his recent brilliant successes in battles and the treaties that followed them, to the glory of France, she never really would do more than understand that the world judged him exceptional – Josephine was beginning to appreciate Napoleon's human qualities: his tenderness and care for her, his affection for her children, his generosity in foreseeing what she might want. This was not a marriage that should bring suffering to her family, and for this she was immediately grateful.

But she did not like the discomforts and dangers involved in travelling as a general's wife close to the front line. When the Austrians, under General Wurmser, advanced on Verona, where the Bonapartes were then staying, Napoleon sent her to Peschiera. There, the horrified General Guillaume, expecting to be attacked any minute, said she could not stay. Josephine, with one of those unexpected touches of obstinacy that came in moments of terror, refused to move without her husband's permission. Bonaparte, hearing of the Austrians' advance, sent Junot to bring her out. No sooner had they left the city than they were fired on by an Austrian gun-boat on Lake Garda: two horses and one of the escort were killed. Junot stopped the coach and pulled Josephine and her maid into a ditch, which he made them run along until the coach was out of range of the guns; then he commandeered a peasant's cart for them. Josephine held back her tears until Napoleon held out his arms to help her down from the cart in Castelnuovo: then, like an overwrought child, she dissolved in his embrace. 'Wurmser shall pay dearly for your tears', said Bonaparte, and this vendetta he would pursue.

Meanwhile he sent Josephine through Tuscany, towards safety, with Hamelin. It was Hamelin who later recorded that Josephine insisted on calling a halt at Brescia, on the grounds that she was too tired to travel further that night, and that Lieutenant Charles, who was returning from a mission, stopped to join them for dinner there. Later, realizing he had left his hat in the sitting room next to Josephine's bedroom, Hamelin went to retrieve it, but was stopped by a sentry with orders that no one was to enter; these orders were given by 'Mme Bonaparte's maid'. Hamelin continued: 'Then it was that I understood that the heroine of Peschiera had reverted to type – had become again the frivolous and giddy Parisienne.'

The frivolous Parisienne, though she wrote to calm her anxious husband, again failed to write often enough to satisfy him, while the Directory failed to send him the reinforcements he needed against the Austrians, and asked for in each letter to them. He could threaten one correspondent better than the other, and he wrote: 'Beware, Josephine! Some fine night the door will burst open and I shall be there in front of you!' But he would have found her alone in her bleak magnificence in Milan, for whatever Hamelin's suspicions, and whatever point her relationship with Lieutenant Charles had now reached, he was at the front and being mentioned in despatches for gallantry at this moment – by General Bonaparte.

Her husband's frenzied letters seemed to Josephine no absolute proof of love: perhaps their torrid quality seemed to her exaggerated and even made her doubt him, for she now asked General Berthier to report to her (from October 1796) about Napoleon. 'Bonaparte loves you truly; do not spurn his tender feelings', wrote Berthier.

At last, in mid-November, Bonaparte's extraordinary and magnificent charge across the Arcola bridge into devastating enemy fire brought victory, and the re-possession of Verona. With one part of his world under control again, he felt immediately confident about the other part. 'I am re-born,' he wrote triumphantly to his wife, telling her the news, and added the postscript 'Give me news of your little belly'. Were there hopes of pregnancy again? A few days later he wrote:

I am going to bed . . . Good God! How happy I should be if I could be there at your lovable toilet, little shoulder, a little white breast, elastic, very firm; above that, a little face with headscarf à la créole – good enough to eat. You know very well that I have not forgotten the little visits; you know, the little black forest . . . I give it a thousand kisses and wait impatiently for the moment when I shall be there... to live in a Josephine, is to live in Elysium. A kiss on your mouth, your eyes, your shoulder, your breast, everywhere, everywhere.

The letter followed her to Genoa, where she had gone on hearing news of the Arcola victory. Bonaparte himself went to find her in Milan, and arrived at the Serbelloni Palace on Saturday 27 November to find it empty. Raging with frustrated love he sent her a bitter note: 'Do not disturb yourself; go to your pleasures. Happiness is made for you. The whole world is only too happy if it can please you, and only your husband is very, very, unhappy.' The next day he wrote again: 'It is not my intention that you should change your plans, nor the parties which are offered you... when I demanded of you a love that equalled my own, I was wrong; why wish that lace should weigh as much as gold?'

He looked as feverish as he felt, his eyes burning bright and his skin sticking to his bones without the buffer of flesh. He looked burnt out. Berthier even noticed swelling on his head and feared that he would develop erysipelas. He wrote anxiously to Josephine: 'Come – he is ill and gravely upset.'

Josephine came. With her came all her usual sweetness, her insight and understanding, her charming little ways, her ability to sooth the nerves and mind of the potential world conqueror, now aged twenty-seven.

The man she had married was a hero. Three successive counter-offensives launched by the Austrians since the summer of 1796 had now failed, and France had enjoyed some of her most glorious and unexpected victories. These were the foundation for the Treaty of Campo Formio which would be signed with Austria in the summer of 1797 – a treaty that gave both the Rhineland and Belgium to France, and also gave her virtual control of Northern Italy. To commemorate what was perhaps *the* moment of victory, Josephine brought from Paris a pupil of the great David, a young painter called Antoine-Jean Gros, to paint the General as he had looked when he crossed the bridge at Arcola. Her earlier slight fear of her husband now seemed to have disappeared in the understanding of him brought by simple domesticity, a few weeks spent under the same roof. When the painter found it difficult to persuade his subject to stay still for long enough to get a likeness, Josephine simply pulled the General onto her lap and held him there till Gros had time enough.

The young Gros understandably thought his patroness 'the very angel of kindness'. Napoleon's aide-de-camp, Lavalette, said that such familiarities were excused by 'the youth of the happy couple and the artist's . . . enthusiasm for the hero'. He also noted: 'The commander-in-chief was, at that time, supremely happy in his wife's company. Mme Bonaparte was charming, and not all the worries of high command, not all the responsibilities of government, could stop her husband enjoying that domestic bliss.' In his wife's company Bonaparte could become a different person, as the French ambassador, who spent two wonderful days with them at Lake Maggiore, noticed: '. . . on the road the General proved to be a gay and lively companion, entertaining us with stories of his early life. He showered his wife with attentions, and indulged himself in such conjugal liberties that he continually embarrassed us.'

Another fleeting picture of Josephine, as ever emotionally vulnerable, volatile, and unable to hide her feelings, comes from a young French poet and playwright, Carrion de Nisas: 'Mme Bonaparte is neither young nor pretty, but she is extremely modest and engaging. She often caresses her husband, who seems devoted to her. She frequently weeps, several times a day, for very trivial reasons . . .'

How very different Josephine was from all the women in Napoleon's own family, who could withstand fear and danger without flinching. Where they were proud, fierce, and demanding, she was sweet, submissive, and sympathetic. Alone and with others, General Bonaparte and his wife indulged themselves in a physical and emotional idyll. Their honeymoon year had been fraught with separations, suspicions, distractions, danger, the growing knowledge for each of how very different the other was; yet together they could waive all their difficulties; together, with his passion and her response, they made up the balance of love. He was becoming her Empire.

5. Scandal International

In Italy Napoleon began to appreciate, objectively, the charm that Josephine exerted over others as well as himself. Now that he was in possession of her, jealousy gave way to pride as he announced '*Je ne gagne que les batailles; Josephine me gagne les coeurs*' (I only win battles; Josephine wins hearts for me).

But, with the exception of her husband's, Josephine would never even touch the fringes of any Bonaparte heart, and of this she quickly became aware as Napoleon's family streamed into Milan. First came sixteen-year-old Pauline, the striking beauty of the family, chosen as a model by Canova, who even years later displayed her exquisitely slender body to her ladies-in-waiting every day after one of the frequent baths to which the whole Bonaparte family, like Josephine, was addicted. She was known as the most beautiful woman of her time, but she had a mean nature. From the first she hated Josephine, and would stick out her tongue behind her elegant back, uncaring that Josephine was homesick for France and for her children in the middle of all this splendour, and equally negligent of her own brother's happiness: to cause havoc in the marriage was all she hoped for. Napoleon, who loved his little sister but saw her faults, arranged for her to marry General Leclerc, and for the June ceremony in 1797 her mother Letizia, her sisters Elisa and Caroline, and her brothers Louis and Jerome, arrived to add their weight to the dislike that Joseph, Lucien and Pauline already had for Josephine. Josephine's own behaviour, now and in all her dealings with the Bonapartes, was impeccable, and years later, on St Helena, Napoleon complimented her on it when talking to an aide: 'She lavished courtesy and attentions on her mother-in-law, and was equally considerate of her sisters-in-law.'

In June, the month of Pauline's marriage, Napoleon promoted Hippolyte Charles to the rank of captain in the First Hussars. Before long, Pauline's incorrigibly roving eye was taken by Charles, but when she saw where his real interest lay, she quickly alerted her brother. According to Laure Permon, 'the situation was known to all the army... Charles appeared

86

Jerome, the youngest of the Bonaparte brothers

*Like the rest of the Bonapartes,
Pauline was addicted to baths; but
only she took them so publicly. This
is one of the statues of her by Canova*

*Lucien Bonaparte thought his brother
Napoleon a potential "tyrant", and
waged a vicious campaign against
Josephine and Hortense*

as a luncheon guest at the Serbelloni Palace as soon as the general left the city . . . if only a tender friendship it occupied much of [Josephine's] time.'

Gossip had also linked Josephine's name with the two Generals, Murat and Junot, whom Napoleon had despatched to Paris to fetch her more than a year ago, and one day when Josephine was playing *vingt-et-un* with Junot, her husband crept in and seized Junot's hair so savagely that a half-healed wound sprang open and drenched Napoleon's hands with blood. Junot (later to marry Laure Permon) had in fact paid more attention to the maid than the mistress in the travelling coach that had brought them all – Junot, Joseph Bonaparte, Hippolyte Charles, and Hamelin – to Italy with Josephine and her maid, Louise Compoint, and Josephine had finally, after putting up with a degree of insolence, taken the unusual step of dismissing the girl. According to Napoleon himself, it was the maid's accusation, and not all the gossip passed on by his family, that convinced him that Josephine might be unfaithful. It was, as he said, 'a confidence I could have well done without'.

It was from Rastadt, where Napoleon was ratifying the peace treaty in November 1797, that an order was suddenly despatched ordering the newly promoted captain to return to Paris forthwith. Then, in answer to a summons to himself from the Directory, Napoleon himself set out for Paris through Switzerland, the quickest way. Josephine had been waiting for her husband in Venice, but hearing of his departure for Paris she, too, set off for home.

She was not preceded, but apparently followed, by Captain Charles: Berthier had failed to pass the Commander-in-Chief's curt order on, and instead issued a softer directive, giving him three months leave to 'settle some family affairs'. The Captain left Milan on 22 December.

By then Bonaparte had already been in Paris for more than two weeks. He had arrived home on 5 December to find that Josephine's orders, despatched from Italy, for her little house in the rue Chantereine to be redecorated 'in the latest elegance' had been carried out with such zeal that the bill for the work came to more than three times the worth of the building itself! With

Photo Bulloz

Reconstruction of the bedroom in the rue Chantereine which Josphine had decorated in military style for Napoleon

its tent-like bedroom, its occasional tables looking like drums, its twin beds apparently mounted on cannon, which sprang together at the touch of a lever, it was all planned to be immensely flattering to the conquering hero; and the Paris crowds added their own touch, demanding that the street should be renamed 'rue de La Victoire'.

But where, again, was Josephine? She was inching her way home on yet another treacherous journey, across the Alps. When she reached the French roads there were fêtes for her in all the big towns. In Paris, Talleyrand had planned a spectacular reception for her. As she did not arrive when she was expected, he had to plan it three separate times, each time sending out first invitations and then cancellations, and throwing away the forests of flowers – in winter – that had been ordered. Finally, on 2 January, Josephine arrived in Paris, after another journey that the gossips would turn against her.

The next evening, Talleyrand finally brought off his magnificent reception in the Hôtel Galliflet. Josephine wore a Greek tunic and her hair, which was always dressed with

89

fantastic imagination for evenings like this, was caught up with a fillet of laurels. Bonaparte, surprisingly, was in civilian clothes. One of the guests noticed that he seemed possessive with his wife and madly in love with her.

Another guest was Talleyrand's own former mistress, the formidable Germaine de Staël, daughter of the former French Finance Minister, Necker. She asked Napoleon,

'General, which is the woman you love the most?'

'My wife.'

'Of course, but which is the one you could admire the most?'

'She who runs her household best.'

'I see that too. But which would you consider the First among women?'

'She who bore most children, Madame.'

Mme de Staël tried a last thrust: 'They say you don't like women very much.' Napoleon was ready: 'Pardon me, Madame, I love the one I married very much.'

Josephine was hurt by the allusion to children: she knew by now his passion for children, his love for hers, his desire for his own; and after more than two years, admittedly spent mainly apart, she was still not pregnant.

The geographical and emotional difficulties of this relationship were closely intertwined. It was not until now, January 1798, that Napoleon had a chance to level his own questions to Josephine about her supposedly having stayed at the same inns as the then Lieutenant Charles on the way to Italy. (Napoleon still did not know that the same story would soon circulate about her journey from Italy to Paris.)

He remembered later having been fairly gentle with her: 'Tell the truth, there's no great harm in that, and then one can travel together stay at the same inns without...'

But she interrupted him with tears and a distraught 'No, it's not true' – always, he noted, her first reaction under attack: not, as he saw it, usually a deliberate lie, but a form of self-defence.

In March Captain Charles resigned his commission. He was building a new career, with the help of Josephine and her old patrons, in the Lyons-based Bodin Company which was receiving contracts to supply provisions to the Army of Italy.

90

The arrangement (which was later said to be the origin of Charles's fortune) smelt of intrigue and corruption, and it was Joseph Bonaparte, now ambassador to Rome, who brought the bad news to Napoleon.

This time, evidently, the interrogation was not so gentle: it was conducted by Napoleon and Joseph together, no doubt behaving like avenging twins in a Corsican mafia. Josephine was always stupid about money, but the other elements in this affair left her with no defence if she were found guilty.

She poured out her shock in an overwrought, near-hysterical letter to Charles. (This was undated but was probably in the last week of March.)

Napoleon asked me whether I knew the Citizen Bodin, whether it was I who had procured for him the purveyor's contract with the Army of Italy ... and whether it was true that Charles was lodging at the Citizen Bodin's house at 100 rue du Faubourg St Honoré. I replied that I knew nothing of what he was talking about; if he wanted a divorce he had only to say so ... Yes, my Hippolyte, they have all my hate; you alone have my tenderness, my love; they must know how much I detest them by the frightful state I have been in for several days; they see the regret, the despair, I feel at being deprived of seeing you as often as I wish. Hippolyte, I shall kill myself; yes, I want to put an end to a life that would always be a burden to me if it could not be devoted to you ... What have I done to these monsters? ...

She had learned a great deal from Napoleon's letters, but the suicide threat was overtaken in a succeeding paragraph where she promised to let him know tomorrow what time she could meet Charles in the Mousseau Garden – now the Parc Monceau. She ended with a thousand 'burning kisses'.

This letter, with its admission of lies and intended deceits and its childish frenzy, reveals Josephine at her very worst. Her loyalty to Charles, and indirectly to her own safety, weighs little against this. It also contains some contradictions: one would have expected her to rejoice at the thought of divorce

91

from 'these monsters', but perhaps the plural is the clue: as a clan she hated the Bonapartes, although she never showed this to them; individually, she was by now at least extremely fond of Napoleon. But as for being in love, why that, plainly, could only be with Charles himself. It is hard then to see how or why she should have resisted him as a lover.

Napoleon, then, had made his wife promise not to see Hippolyte Charles again. But even after his discovery of the Bodin contract, even though Louise Compoint and his sister had pointed accusing fingers at Josephine, he did not give way completely to the suspicions others found for him and that, with his jealous nature, could have ruled him. Instead, he carried on with preparations for his campaign in Egypt: he felt his glory in France was fading and needed fresh victories to feed it.

Pauline must have felt frustrated at seeing the flames she tried so hard to fan dowsed, in retrospect, by Napoleon's capacity for independent thought, and Josephine's promise not to see Charles. But she had at least the satisfaction of seeing her suffer. 'My sister-in-law nearly died of vexation,' she told Laure Permon jubilantly. 'Now, you know that we do not die of vexation merely at being parted from our friends, so there must have been more than mere friendship in that relationship. As for me, I tried to comfort my brother, who was exceedingly unhappy. He was aware of the situation . . . before he went to Egypt.' But even he knew that many of his past suspicions had been unfounded, that his family hated Josephine, that they were malicious where she, if self-centred, was forgiving.

In March he bought the house that was still their home, in the re-named rue de la Victoire. In May they travelled from Paris to Toulon: Napoleon intended Josephine to join him in Egypt as soon as his successes made this safe. Meanwhile she would go to Plombières to take the waters, famed for encouraging fertility.

But Josephine had been deeply shaken by the bare sight of the Bonapartes' hatred for her, and the thought of being separated from Napoleon filled her with foreboding. Separation had always brought trouble between them, whereas together they could be wonderfully happy. When the time came for

Napoleon to sail, Josephine was in tears. There was nothing better she could have done: Napoleon wanted to be loved by women as much as he wanted to rule men, and later in his life he would express tenderness to mistresses, not because he loved them, but because they loved him.

On the six weeks voyage to Egypt, he was raving about his wife once more. 'In our private conversations, Josephine was almost always the subject . . . his attachment to her bordered on idolatry,' remembered Bourrienne, the secretary who sailed with him.

Meanwhile Josephine wrote to Barras: 'I am so unhappy to be separated from him that I have a sadness I cannot overcome . . ., his brother, with whom he corresponds so closely, behaves so badly towards me that I am always anxious when I am far from Bonaparte.' She added, 'I love him well, for all his little faults.' But her love was still very self-centred, as was revealed when she later said to Barras: 'I have received a charming letter from Bonaparte. He says that he can't live without me.'

Napoleon wanted her to set sail from Naples to join him, but she was recovering from an injury – well authenticated this time – sustained when a balcony she was standing on with some friends in Plombières collapsed and she fell twenty feet into the street. The pain was severe, the voyage delayed. But in the late summer, after celebrating Napoleon's many successes in Egypt, she heard of Nelson's victory at Aboukir Bay on 1 August. She could not now join Bonaparte: and even if she had it might have already been too late.

On 25 July 1798 Bonaparte had written to the brother he still trusted, adding nothing to the news of the victories to date, but saying: 'I have great private unhappiness; the veil has finally fallen from my eyes . . . Arrange for me to have a country house when I get back, either near Paris or in Burgundy; I intend to shut myself up there for the winter: I have had enough of human nature. I need solitude and quiet; grandeur bores me; my emotions are dried up . . . all that is left for me is to become a complete egotist.'

This was not the anger of suspicion or jealousy, but the depression of the betrayed and disillusioned: a disgust with human frailty, with people, with the prizes of the world; the need of a sick soul to heal itself in solitude.

The most worried witness of the General's state of mind was Josephine's son, sixteen-year-old Eugène Beauharnais, who was accompanying Bonaparte on this, his own first, campaign. The letter that he wrote to her and Napoleon's to Joseph were both intercepted by the British and added to the Bonapartes' marital difficulties, but here is evidence both of the cause of Napoleon's grief and of his extreme fairness and love in dealing with Eugène himself:

My dear Mama,

I have so much to tell you that I don't know where to begin. Bonaparte has appeared extremely sad for five days, after a conversation with Julien, Junot and Berthier. This talk has affected him more than I thought. From what I have heard it amounts to this: that Charles travelled in your coach until you were within three posting stations of Paris; that you saw him in Paris; that you were with him in the private boxes at the Theatre of the Italians; that he gave you your little dog; that even now he is close to you; that is all I have been able to gather from snatches of conversation. You know, Mama, that I don't believe this, but what is certain is that the General is deeply affected by it. However, he redoubles his friendship for me. He seems, by his actions, to say that children are not responsible for the faults of their mother . . .

To Napoleon's relief the jealous Fortuné had died, but he had indeed been replaced by another little dog given to Josephine by Hippolyte Charles.

Why should General Bonaparte, in Egypt, suddenly believe what he had refused to countenance for so long when passed on by his brother, his sister, and Josephine's former maid? It seems probable that he had been able to convince himself that their accusations were malicious, prompted by the desire for revenge on Josephine; but that he was unable to attribute such a motive to the present informants; Junot particularly was an old and loved friend. There was also the sheer weight of accumulated evidence.

An account of what was most probably the same conversation (though wrongly dated in his account) comes in Bourrienne's *Memoirs*. He saw Junot and Napoleon walking together, and suddenly noticed the latter change colour and strike his own head violently. Then in savage snatches he vent his emotions: 'You do not care for me at all. If you did you would have told me what I have just heard from Junot; there stands a true friend. Josephine! And I 600 leagues away! You should have told me! Josephine! to have deceived me thus! She! Woe upon them! I shall exterminate this race of whipper-snappers and fops . . . As for Her – a divorce! Yes, divorce, a public and open divorce! . . .'

Both Napoleon's letter to Joseph about his private unhappiness and Eugène's letter to his mother were published by the Cabinet in London, a fact deplored by the *Morning Chronicle* on 24 November. The French press quickly reprinted the *Chronicle*'s leading article, which gave a good indication of the contents of the letters to an avid audience in Paris. So a private despair had become a public scandal, and one that enemy governments sought to profit by. How could a man so concerned with his own glory, a man so proud, a *Corsican*, ever live happily after such a disclosure?

Josephine must indeed have wondered what Napoleon had in store for her now. His reaction in Egypt was fairly prompt and predictable. First he had six Asiatic women sent in for his inspection. Finding them too fat for his fastidious taste, they were just as arbitrarily dismissed. Then he saw the charming little Pauline Fourès, a blonde with hair long enough to cover all the lovely skin on her neat little body, who had been smuggled into Egypt by her new husband, a lieutenant. The Lieutenant quickly found himself posted elsewhere, while his bride seemed only too happy to respond to his General's wishes.

Eugène, who had listened to some of Napoleon's sad out-pourings, was now required to ride behind the carriage carrying the General and the woman with whom he was revenging himself on his mother. The boy asked for a transfer,

Photo Bulloz

Photo Bulloz

Malmaison seen from the park behind

Caesar's wife : Josephine drawing the First Consul

Josephine's bedroom at Malmaison, with the bed in which she died

Photo Bulloz

but, after a heated scene, Napoleon's feeling for family took precedence: the public drives came to an end.

Almost another year was to elapse before Napoleon's return from Egypt, and for Josephine, notwithstanding what must have been the acute embarrassment of the published letters, it was an eventful and not altogether unhappy time. She was now most distinguished as a hostess, and her guest lists contained what was, in this curious post-revolutionary society, the cultural as well as the political *crème de la crème*: not only the Directors and the leading beauties but the greatest living French painters, writers, and musicians.

One of her new close friends was Mme Gohier, whose husband Louis was elected to the Directory in June 1799. Two months previously Josephine had finally acquired what she and Bonaparte had both independently wanted, and had discussed buying jointly before he sailed to Egypt: a country house. It was the charming house of Malmaison, with its own farm, about eight miles outside Paris, that Josephine bought. Most of the money for this expensive purchase was probably advanced to her by Barras.

Some thought, and some hoped, that her husband might never return. Claire de Rémusat remembers that her mother, who had known Josephine at Croissy, met her again when visiting a friend near Malmaison: 'Bonaparte was considered virtually lost to France; his wife was neglected. My mother felt sorry for her and we showed her some kindnesses; she has never forgotten them. At that time I was seventeen, and had been married for a year.' Hortense, with whom Claire was to become friendly, was nearly three years younger.

In general, society was tending to turn its back on Josephine now that her husband's star was no longer obviously in the ascendant. 'Since I have lived in the country, I have become such a recluse that the outside world frightens me,' she wrote to Barras in September. But after an isolated start, Malmaison was to be the happiest of Josephine's houses, her truest home, and some of her first happy days there were spent with Hippolyte Charles. They were days of reconciliation, since their relationship had been under some strain earlier in the year.

The Gohiers, concerned about Bonaparte's reaction if he should return to France and hear more gossip about his wife, recommended discretion to her. When Josephine protested that she could not refuse to see Charles, and anyway that there was nothing but friendship between them, Gohier answered cannily that a friendship so exclusive was as much an argument for Josephine to seek a divorce as a great love would have been. But Josephine would not apparently even consider divorce.

On 10 October 1799 the Gohiers gave a dinner party. A message arrived there for Josephine: Bonaparte had landed at Fréjus. She told Gohier, by now an admirer, 'I am going to meet him. It is important for me to reach him ahead of his brothers, who have always hated me.' Then, turning to his wife, she added, with her inimitable charm, 'When Bonaparte learns, Madame, that it is with you that I spent my time while he was away, he will be flattered as well as grateful . . .'

The next morning she set out at dawn to drive south with Hortense. She took the eastern Burgundy route with her daughter, while Napoleon, driving north with her son, took the west road, the Bourbonnais. By the time she had realized her error and corrected it, he was in Paris two days ahead of her. As Eugène wrote, 'Sufficient time for her enemies!'

The Bonapartes, her enemies, rushed to greet him, and, according to the account later given by Laure Permon, Josephine's absence was construed as guilt. Having reported to the Directory, Napoleon told as many of them as were interested, and some other friends, that she should not set foot in his house again. Most tried to calm him, and a financier, Jean-Pierre Collot, added some shrewd persuasion: at the end of a tirade, he said, 'Such violence on your part convinces me that you are still in love with her.' He predicted that Josephine would be forgiven, and peace restored.

Two days later Josephine arrived in the night to find her husband's door bolted against her. Through it he told her that she must leave. She implored him but he remained implacable. Hortense and Eugène came up the little narrow back staircase where she was by now lying prostrate, and added their pleas to hers. The door remained closed. At last, at about 4 a.m., the three of them gave up, and prepared to retreat. The effect on Napoleon was probably much the same as his proposed departure had been on Josephine before they married. By his own account (told to Collot) he said, 'Just as she was leaving, going down the stairs in tears, I saw Hortense and Eugène go after her, sobbing too. I was not born with a heart in my bosom that could stand the sight and sound of tears.' He reached out first to the boy he had learned to love so much, and then Hortense and her mother were in his arms too.

Napoleon sent not for Joseph, of whom he remained fond as yet, but for Lucien, who of all his brothers was capable of the greatest malice. It was 7 a.m. He instructed that nothing should be sent to prepare him: Lucien presented himself, and found husband and wife in bed together.

From her Corsican vantage-point, Laure Permon judged: 'Whatever his wife's errors might be, Bonaparte appeared to forget them entirely, and the reconciliation was complete. Of all the members of the family, Mme Leclerc [Pauline] was the most annoyed at the pardon Napoleon had granted his wife. Bonaparte's mother was also ill-pleased, but she said nothing.'

Before long, and then for several years, Napoleon would find domestic wars far more troublesome than his conquest and reorganization of Europe. In the end he lamented at St Helena: 'I never received any cooperation from my family . . . It was sufficient for me to make one of my brothers a king for him to believe at once that it was by the grace of God. He became not a lieutenant on whom I could lean, but another enemy that I had to watch out for.' But before he could make his brothers kings, Bonaparte had to assume more powers.

He had returned from his campaigns in Egypt and Syria to a France that was threatened on all sides. War had broken out again in March of the same year (1799): the Austrians had entered Milan and taken back Northern Italy, with Russian support, and more Russians had invaded Switzerland, while another Austrian Army was advancing through the Black Forest. It seemed to the General that he could not leave his country in other hands without disaster overtaking it: this was a situation he must remedy.

6. Caesar's Wife

Josephine's role as a muse of victory was clearly understood by the shrewdest of her observers, Claire de Rémusat. 'What a situation for a woman to find herself in – as one of the motivating influences for the triumphal march of a whole army!' she marvelled. But Mme de Rémusat was also quick to discern the undertones of brooding jealousy and disillusionment that ran through some of Napoleon's most impassioned letters to his wife, and wondered whether Josephine did not also, through her initial carelessness, play another role: by damaging Bonaparte's early, idealistic conception of love, she asked, did she wreck his final capacity for emotional fulfilment? 'Perhaps the disappointments . . . took their toll, made their mark, and blighted, one by one, his capacity for love. Perhaps he would have been a better man had he been more, and above all better, loved.'

If so, Josephine could have been mainly responsible for the growth of that element of tyranny in her husband, noticed by Lucien while he was still a lieutenant, which gained ground in his personality as he aged. But Claire de Rémusat, who read the letters to Josephine, had not seen those other early writings, which showed an adolescent soul, in doubt and sometimes pain, but nevertheless determined to impose its own solutions on the world. The Egyptian campaign had been a watershed in the Bonapartes' relationship: Napoleon, with his strong sense of justice (often admittedly rather rough), would never again permit himself to be entirely ruled by, or be faithful to, a wife who, as well as being more womanly than most members of her sex, had more than her fair share of womanly frailty. But the most complicated years of their relationship were still ahead of them.

Napoleon was triply tied to Josephine, by affection, need, and superstition. 'He was convinced that I brought him luck, and nothing would induce him to start on a campaign without previously kissing me,' Josephine once admitted of Napoleon. He had always had a strong sense of destiny, thought that his 'lucky star' had saved him when he was imprisoned after Robespierre's fall, and, in his heart, agreed with the crowds who called Josephine 'Notre Dame des Victoires'.

Now, between his return to Paris on 16 October, and '18 Brumaire' (9 November) 1799 he had less than a month to find enough luck and enough support to bring off his most audacious stroke of all: no conventional campaign, but the overthrow of the Directory itself.

He had been spiritually confirmed in his sense of his own destiny a few days after the battle of Lodi on 10 May 1796, two months after his marriage, when he remembered 'I felt the world flying past my feet'. He was able to analyze his feeling exactly: he was in Milan after his victory when a letter arrived from the Directory telling him to hand over his command of the Italian Army to General Kellerman, an order he deemed senseless. He later said: 'From this precise moment dates my conception of my superiority. I felt that I was worth much more and was much stronger than the Government that had seen fit to issue such an order; that I was better fitted than it was to govern; and that the Government was not only incapable but also lacking in judgment on matters that were so important as ultimately to endanger France. I felt that I was destined to save France. From that moment I glimpsed my goal and marched directly towards it.'

The tramp of those ambitious feet was muffled by the cosy domestic peace in the back rooms of the pretty pavilion in the rue de la Victoire. Napoleon did not go out in Paris after his return from the East, but waited for his followers to come to him. Probably only Gohier and his wife, outside the inner circle of conspirators, glimpsed what might lie ahead.

The scene throughout those crucial twenty-three days before the *coup* was one of utter tranquillity and marital bliss. Josephine, now thirty-six, was sitting with Napoleon, to all appearances a soldier completely in repose, at a table in front of the fire one evening, 'alone in the salon, playing at back-gammon', yet another of the many games she enjoyed, and she played it both quickly and well. Some of the conspirators arrived, but Josephine did not retire. She was still, at this stage, very much in her husband's political confidence, and it was

102

later noted that she had been present at every conference. Nor did she merely listen: that acute sensitivity about the feelings, and often the motives, of others was called into play whenever there was the threat of friction, whenever there was a clash of personalities or anxieties, and invariably she restored calm.

Napoleon's own aim was straightforward: he felt that the time had come for him to assume command of the Government. But it was out of the question for him to gain power through legal channels: he was still only thirty, and the minimum age for election to the Directory was forty. It has often proved easier in France to overthrow the machine than to change it. His plot, therefore, was to gain the support of the other senior generals (he largely succeeded), and to persuade at least three of the five Directors to resign, leaving the country without a legally constituted government – the *quorum* was three – whereupon he could assume power. At least two of the Directors, Sieyès and Roger Ducos, were privy to the plot. Napoleon also had the support of Talleyrand, then Minister of Foreign Affairs, and Fouché, the Minister of Police, although both these ex-clerics would prove in time as unfaithful to him as to their religion and every other vow they made. The Minister of Justice, Cambacérès (a great admirer and later a staunch supporter of Josephine) was also pro-Bonaparte. Josephine sent a note to her friend Gohier, the President of the Directory, inviting him to breakfast before the *coup* in the hope of getting his last minute support, but he astutely sidestepped and sent his wife instead. Afterwards, Josephine pleaded his case with Napoleon, and ensured his safety; unlike some she had helped, he always remained grateful.

The *coup* took two days to complete. On 18 *Brumaire* (9 November) one of the conspirators had put a motion to the Council of Ancients* which resulted in the legislature being removed the next day to St Cloud, on the far side of the Bois

* The Council of Five Hundred (Cinq Cents) was composed of 500 members who must be at least 25, although Lucien Bonaparte was only 24 and President of the Council; they proposed, discussed, and moved all draft laws. The Council of Ancients had 250 members aged at least 40: they discussed and voted on all laws passed by the Lower House.

de Boulogne, and the command of all troops in the Paris region being given to General Bonaparte. On 19 *Brumaire* (10 November) Napoleon first addressed the Ancients, with far less than his usual self-confidence, and then went on to speak to the recalcitrant Five Hundred. When he entered the *Orangerie* at St Cloud to speak to them he was shouted down with cries of 'Tyrant'. He was hustled outside to safety, while inside Lucien, only twenty-four but extraordinarily cool, drew his sword and shouted dramatically, 'I swear I will stab my brother through the heart if he ever attempts anything against the Liberty of Frenchmen!'

This promise was given instant leverage by a bayonet charge now led into the Orangerie by Napoleon's present and future brothers-in-law, General Leclerc (Pauline's husband) and General Murat (who married Caroline two months later).

The girls were at the Théâtre Feydeau in Paris with their mother and Mme Permon when an announcement was made from the stage: 'General Bonaparte has only just escaped assassination'. They hurried out and through the crowded streets for news. On reaching the rue de la Victoire they heard that the *coup* had been successful: General Bonaparte had been sworn into power with the title of First Consul; Sieyès and Roger Ducos were to support him. Mme Permon remarked, 'There is a pike who will gobble up the other two fish.' (A few weeks later they were replaced by Cambacérès and Lebrun.)

At four in the morning, Napoleon returned to the rue de la Victoire to celebrate with an anxiously expectant Josephine. 'Tomorrow,' he told her proudly, 'we sleep in the Luxembourg.'

It was in fact four days before they were ready to move into their first State Apartments. Then in February 1800, after a National Referendum had accepted the new Constitution, they moved into the former Royal Palace of the Tuileries. Napoleon told his valet, Constant, that the main thing was not to move in, but to stay there. It was different for Josephine, whose instinctive reaction to the Tuileries was one of distaste. She found it gloomy, and told Hortense: 'I know I shall not be happy here. The darkest forebodings came over me as soon as

I came in.' Perhaps, subconsciously, she realized that power was replacing love as Napoleon's guiding passion.

For a few days she walked through the dark, high-ceilinged rooms with their high sills, overwhelmed with depression and constantly thinking about the fate of Marie Antoinette – she 'saw her tragic figure everywhere' (Mlle Ducrest noticed the same obsession ten years later) – and no doubt wondered whether the words of the fortune-teller would come true, and she herself would be 'killed in a popular commotion'. Napoleon probably did little to improve matters on their first night in residence, when, with a wit that must have grated on her sensibilities just then, he said, 'Come, little Créole, lie down in the bed of your masters'.

However, she soon recovered her spirits sufficiently to turn the family drawing room, where she would receive her morning guests, into a charming background to her own colouring and clothes (her decor was always planned with these in mind). The great receptions took place upstairs.

At these receptions, a new Napoleon was quickly making himself felt, and feared. At thirty, he looked very different from the young soldier of seven or eight years before: even Laure Permon had given up laughing at him (except when he assumed the dress of a private citizen, when he was still 'absolutely laughable') and had to admit that although he made not the slightest claim to elegance, leaving that province entirely to Josephine, 'he was neatness itself'. His once spindly legs had filled out to shapeliness now, above narrow ankles, and although he still changed colour violently under emotion, he had lost the yellow, parchment-like complexion that had probably been the result of poor nutrition. He was very proud of his hands, which were always immaculately manicured, and, like all the Bonapartes, he had excellent teeth; while Josephine, like the Beauharnais, had bad ones, 'like cloves', which she had learned to hide even when she was laughing at one of Hippolyte Charles's incredibly quick jokes. He felt the cold terribly and even in July he would order fires in his room.

One evening, about a month after he became First Consul, the fires were banked high in the Luxembourg for a different reason. Josephine was giving a reception, and as usual her women guests were vying with each other in their revealing dresses. Napoleon ordered more and more logs to be added to the blaze, until one lackey pointed out that he could not wedge even one more piece of wood into the crammed, monumental fireplaces. The First Consul loudly explained that he wanted to make quite sure that his guests were not cold: they were, after all, 'half-naked'. A new fashion was born the next day.

Respectability became a watchword at the Tuileries, outwardly at least. Divorcées and those who had colourful private lives found themselves struck off the guest lists. Perhaps they were fortunate, for those who were admitted had to run the gauntlet of Napoleon's temperament, always erratic, and now taking on an apparently sadistic tinge (the revenge for an unsuccessful adolescence as far as women were concerned?) with his female guests.

Rules were soon laid down that only French fabrics were to be worn in the Tuileries and wherever the First Consul was expected; since most white materials, particularly the flimsy, floating ones beloved by Josephine, were imported from England, a certain amount of cheating was bound to follow such an edict. To assist the silk industry of Lyons, the First Consul himself took the opportunity of ordering some splendid silk costumes. 'I desire you will be dazzling,' he once instructed his wife. 'I will then be superb.'

Thérèse Tallien, to whom he had once, through Barras, sent a kiss 'on the lips', was now no longer among the beauties invited to what was virtually a 'court'. With her string of lovers, husbands, and illegitimate children, Napoleon considered that she was unsuitable company for the First Consul's wife. However, Mlle Ducrest was convinced that Josephine continued to invite her friend secretly to Malmaison, and that Napoleon, who had spies everywhere, chose to ignore the fact: public acquiescence was all that he insisted upon.

He was still more inconsistent over money. While constantly grumbling about her expenditure, and sometimes cutting her dressmaking and milliners' bills arbitrarily by half, he also insisted that Josephine should spend lavishly on clothes and jewels for her public appearances: the Tuileries Palace was daily becoming more regal. Yet Josephine, even with the large allowance given her for clothes, could not make ends meet: she was said to order six hundred dresses a year from the fabulous Leroy and there were times when this figure rose to 900, plus 1,000 pairs of gloves a year. Josephine always changed, to the skin, three times a day, and there were times when she might have three morning appointments of very different kinds for which a change of clothes were necessary, followed by a change for the afternoon and then a *grande toilette* for the evening, when a ball could bring the number of dresses in one day to five. She never wore a pair of stockings twice; she had an accumulation of debts from the past; she was beautifying Malmaison with artificial lakes, glasshouses and aviaries, importing tropical birds and flowers, and stocking a menagerie with kangaroos, chimpanzees, and lions; she was always lavish in presents and trousseaux for her friends, and she gave generously to numbers of charities, public and private. Bourrienne noted, 'Josephine's mania for spending was almost the only cause of her un-happiness. Her creditors were always grumbling and this brought about a highly unfavourable reaction in Paris.'

When Talleyrand swiftly reported the grumbling to Napoleon, he ordered Bourrienne to find out how much Josephine owed altogether. It was 1,200,000 francs, but she told him she would only admit to half of this amount to Napoleon. In vain Bourrienne tried to persuade her that it would be much easier if she declared the full amount. 'I dare not, he is so violent. I know him, Bourrienne, and I cannot stand up to him in his rages,' she admitted. Bourrienne became an accomplice on another occasion. Napoleon had generously given a diamond necklace of Josephine's to his sister, Caroline, as a wedding present. Josephine decided to replace it with a fine pearl neck-lace, but wondered how she could get the new acquisition past Napoleon's all-seeing gaze. Finally she wore it at a reception, and when Napoleon asked her where it came from, she told him that he had often seen it: it was a gift from the Cisalpine Republic. 'Ask Bourrienne,' she added. And Bourrienne, when questioned, truthfully and by pre-arrangement replied that he had certainly seen the necklace before.

At night the First Consul still shared Josephine's bed. During the day, he worked at his immense task of creating a new France, with an entirely new structure, new civil code (the Napoleonic Code), new system of public education, new everything. As Bourrienne saw, 'everything had to be created.' Often Napoleon would rise at six and work non-stop, eating a sparse office lunch at his desk, until dinner: this he liked to eat tête à tête with Josephine, but might only last some fifteen minutes since they both ate so little. Later, ministers were invited to join them on two evenings a week. He liked to go to bed between 10 p.m. and midnight, very often with Josephine reading to him in her mellifluous voice to soothe him to sleep. She would leave her game of cards or backgammon and her new 'ladies-in-waiting' as soon as she was told he had retired, and join him at once.

It was a hard programme, but he allowed himself moments of complete solace and refreshment to counteract the tension and fits of violent indigestion that increasingly afflicted him. Several times a day he would leave his study and walk up the staircase to Josephine's apartment above. After some time with her he would feel strong enough to go back to his plans; if she was not available he would seek relaxation in a steaming bath instead, soaking himself two or three times a day.

It was the same in the summer after the Palace of St Cloud had been reopened: 'If he had so much as a few free minutes between conferences or appointments,' recorded Claire de Rémusat, 'he came to spend them with Josephine, often rushing in across the terrace at the Palace . . .' Should he find her with friends, he would often just glare sulkily and retreat without another word.

They went increasingly to Malmaison, the First Consul joining the family there for the so-called 'weekends' that, with the new calendar, fell only once every ten days. Here on the grass they all played wild games of 'prisoner's base' and leapfrog, Napoleon rushing about madly with Eugène and Hortense and the young guests. They complied with Napoleon's known preference for pale dresses, and Laure Permon noted, 'the white

108

dress was a uniform for the women at Malmaison . . . Napoleon loved that place passionately.' Josephine, who knew better than anyone that his romantic ideal was to see a tall, slender, graceful figure in a white gown walking along winding garden paths, had planned a sinuous paradise in the garden at Malmaison. She 'almost always wore India muslin, filmy as a cloud', and would walk through the gardens picking some of the exquisite roses she had tended – she looked after favourite blooms herself. Or she might be found inspecting the new tulip bulb for which she had paid 3,000 francs, or looking in the greenhouse at her exotic fruits, including the one pineapple that was ripening there, or rather nervously watching the lions at feeding time. When the weather was bad they played games, and it was difficult to beat Josephine at cards, backgammon or billiards. When it was fine, dinner might be taken *al fresco* on the lawn, to the enjoyment of everyone except Talleyrand, who suffered from rheumatism and said sourly 'The man always thinks he's camping out'.

Life at Malmaison was idyllic, idyllically normal. Here was the generous and fun-loving family atmosphere Napoleon had always dreamed of, but had never, since early childhood, found among his own increasingly spiteful and grasping brothers and sisters. He would never, except in fleeting moments, find such happiness anywhere away from Josephine, Eugène and Hortense, who loved each other so deeply and who now also, all three in their different ways, loved him. Bourrienne reflected, rightly, 'Nowhere, unless perhaps it was on the field of battle, have I ever seen Bonaparte as happy as in the gardens of Malmaison.'

It was from this happiness, and from his appreciation of the Beauharnais qualities – the Beauharnais who were all to remain loyal to him when another wife, and most members of his own family, had deserted him – that Napoleon's ever-deepening love and esteem for them sprang. It was this appreciation that in turn would lead Letizia to lament 'the triumph of a foreign family over my own'. The Beauharnais were so nearly his own family now, and they would indeed have been the perfect family for him: it was a tragedy that Eugène was not his own son, and with only some twelve years between them he felt he could not name him his heir.

When these weekends came to an end, even Napoleon disliked returning to the city, while for the country-bred Josephine and for her children the dismal Tuileries held still less attraction. One day Hortense asked if she might stay on with Mme Campan in St Germain instead of returning to Paris with the others. Josephine looked tearful, and the lover in Napoleon came out at once. Hortense remembered:

He pulled my mother on to his lap, holding her tight in his arms, accusing her, in a tone half serious, half bantering, of 'loving your children more than you do me'. 'It's not true,' my mother replied. 'You cannot doubt my devotion, but without my children around me my happiness is incomplete.' 'What can be missing from it,' the Consul asked, 'When you have a husband, as good as any, who loves only you, children who bring you only pleasure? Come – admit that you're a very fortunate woman.' 'You're right, it's true, I am,' my mother admitted, all smiles, whereas a minute before she had been all tears.

Yet there was enough of his own family in Napoleon, superior as he was to the rest in most ways, to make him very difficult to live with at times. There were the 'funny little ways' that Josephine had mentioned to Barras, the increasingly common and terrifying rages, and now, in spite of the newly cleansed Consular society, from which divorcées and deep décolletages were alike excluded, there were the mistresses.

Napoleon had not seen Pauline Fourès since his return from Egypt, although he had made sure that she was well provided for and given a pension. Josephine did not seem to have taken this geographically distant infidelity to heart; in fact, Claire de Rémusat noted that she used the name Fourès to good effect whenever the question of her own fertility came up. Napoleon had never fathered a child, so who could be sure that it was her fault that they had none, when she was the mother of two?

Now, perhaps partly in an attempt to discover whether he was

110

capable of producing his own heir, but much more because he was seized by the needs of his own flesh, and thought increasingly that he was above the laws that bound other men, Napoleon brought his mistresses closer and closer to his home.

France's defeat by Austria and Russia had looked imminent when Napoleon returned from Egypt, but already in spite of the new administrative chaos inside the country, French troops were acquitting themselves better. Napoleon's next campaign, which he always regarded as exemplary, was to reach fulfilment in the battle of Marengo. His plan in the spring of 1800 was simply to leave a force holding the front against the enemy while he led a second force across the Alps and attacked from the rear, catching the enemy in a pincer movement. It worked.

Napoleon retired to Milan once more to celebrate victory, and met again the famous singer La Grassini, the prima donna of La Scala, who was now twenty-seven. She had made no secret of her attraction to him four years before, but at that time both his reputation and Josephine had been so much in the balance that either could have escaped him. Now he felt secure in both, and, by her more obvious dependence on him, his wife had removed the challenge that had constituted a major element in his early obsession with her. Again it was a voice that drew him: Bourrienne recollected that Napoleon could have listened to La Grassini singing for hours. She was also a handsome and experienced woman, and one who was very much used to having her own way. When Napoleon commanded her to come to Paris, she obeyed; but when she found that she was to play a supporting role, waiting quietly and alone in the wings until he was ready to send for her, she quickly found a lover, a violinist, with more time to devote to her and made good her escape. But, brief though her stay was, it upset the Consular household: Josephine wrote to her friend Mme de Krény saying that she and Napoleon were having a terrible scene every day, which she attributed to her rival's presence in the city, and that she could not go on living like this. She also pointed out, in a tone that was new, but was surely the result of the terrible scene the year before when she and her children had stood outside Napoleon's locked door, that she was herself now quite blameless. She could no longer keep Napoleon on tenterhooks: the past evidence against her was too weighty for her to risk even the most innocent flirtation again. Her only chance lay in unimpeachable fidelity.

She was indeed now Caesar's wife, and would become still more obviously so in August 1802 when Napoleon was created Consul for Life and granted the privilege, like the Caesars, of naming his own heir. But temperamentally Josephine was not suited to this role: she disliked both the exaggerated grandeur and the danger attached to it. On Christmas Eve 1800, they were to hear Haydn's *Creation* at the Opera, in a mixed party of family and friends. Napoleon set off with three generals in one coach, and the ladies, Josephine, Caroline Murat and Hortense, followed in the next. Suddenly there was a terrible explosion: an 'infernal machine', a barrel filled with gunpowder, hidden in a cart on the road, had exploded and had narrowly missed them. The party continued to the Opera, where Caroline Murat, who was expecting her first child, kept her iron composure as if nothing had happened, while Josephine shivered in a cashmere shawl and could not hide her tears, nor her anxiety for Napoleon, at whom she kept darting pitiful glances.

Such danger increased the public demand for security of government: Joseph and Lucien Bonaparte saw their chance for greater personal power if their brother were proved sterile, and Lucien suggested that Napoleon should marry the thirteen-year-old Infanta Isabella. There was talk, too, of Napoleon being made king, which would also increase the likelihood of the divorce for which the Bonapartes were hoping so fervently.

Josephine's health had never been robust, and now she was suffering regularly from paralyzing migraines. Laure Permon, whose marriage to General Junot had recently been arranged by Napoleon, was now a regular visitor to Malmaison, and noticed other signs of strain. Josephine was beginning to wear powder for the first time, and Napoleon teased her about it until he brought tears to her eyes; then, as usual at the sight of tears, he repented.

Another time he forced her, in a carriage, to 'jump' a stream, or as it seemed to her a precipice, which had steep banks but no

Hortense, daughter of Josephine, later wife of Louis Bonaparte and Queen of Holland

Photo Bulloz

Napoleon in about 1802, by David

Photo Bulloz

bridge. 'This is absolute childishness,' he said, 'You *shall* go over.' And seeing the coachman hesitate, he gave him a lash across the shoulders with his whip. (To make matters worse, he allowed Laure, who was pregnant, to descend from the carriage first, on the grounds that the jolt might injure her child.) The carriage lurched across violently. One of the carriage springs broke, Josephine shrieked and sobbed, Bonaparte felt furious (and perhaps guilty) and dragged her into a wood to tell her off. When she said he must love someone else: 'You are a fool, and if you repeat that I shall say you are a wicked fool, because you do not think what you are saying. You know how I hate these senseless jealousies. You will end by putting it into my head. Now! Kiss me and hold your tongue. You are ugly when you cry – I have told you so before.'

Mortified, Josephine covered her face with her veil for the silent drive back.

Reports of such scenes as these were bound to travel fast and far, as no one now realized better than Josephine. She took care therefore to write to her mother saying she was to believe only the news she herself sent. In October 1801 she wrote: 'He makes your daughter very happy; he is good, kind, a charming man in every way. He loves your Yeyette.'

In comparison with Alexandre, all this was true. But what was obvious now was that the memory of the extreme passion she had once evoked in Napoleon, and the realization that she had been slow to recognize many of his excellent qualities, to love him back to the full when he most needed it, had aroused a rather painful love in her now, when she felt he was less dependent on her. The painter Isabey, as observant of behaviour as of appearance, was worried. 'Josephine was completely submissive to her husband's ascendancy. I noticed with concern that her affection for him seemed to increase, while the General's love for her was diminishing as time went on.' Isabey was called upon more and more frequently to perfect Josephine's always exquisite makeup.

Josephine's excessive concern with her appearance, and her jealousies, for which there was often no cause at all and certainly no serious cause at this time, were reflections of her insecurity,

114

which in turn was caused by her desperate concern about the succession. This was made still worse by another fruitless journey to Plombières in the summer of 1801. If she could not produce an heir for Napoleon, someone else must – yet she instinctively shied away from a scheme of Lucien's either for her to get a child by another man or to let Napoleon father one elsewhere and adopt it. In the end, it was her beloved Hortense who was sacrificed: the most selfish and desperate act of Josephine's life, and one that would bring her sorrow and her daughter desolation. Hortense was to be married to Louis, the brother for whom Napoleon, having found out some of the faults of the others, retained most affection. The eighteen-year-old Hortense had already refused several good matches, because though she might have felt attraction or affection, she did not feel the passionate love that she looked for in marriage. Now she deliberately agreed to a loveless marriage (on her side at least), simply to help her mother. 'My consent given, I grew calm,' she remembered later. 'All the anguish I had experienced earlier seemed to transfer itself to my mother. She never stopped crying.'

She was right, for Louis was a depressed, introverted, jealous man, who as a husband became a hated tyrant. Lucien proudly declared that he had sown the deadly seeds of the forthcoming saga when he told Louis, just before the wedding, that Hortense was already pregnant by Napoleon. The bride was informed that her husband would never see her again if the child were born within nine months: perhaps unfortunately it was not; but later, when Napoleon wanted to adopt the baby as his heir, the brothers would threaten to reveal the 'scandal' of the birth.

Josephine was thrilled that she was to become a grandmother, but made yet another trip to Plombières herself, at the age of thirty-nine, and feeling very insecure. She was afraid that Napoleon would conceive a passion for someone else similar to his passion for her, which was in fact the last thing in the world he wanted. To have loved once to the verge of madness was quite enough for a man who wanted to rule, not to be ruled. Some time later he told Claire de Rémusat in some irritation:

'Josephine is always afraid that I will really fall in love. She fails to comprehend that love is not for me. For what is love, after all, but a passion which casts all the rest of the universe aside to concentrate, wholly, solely and exclusively, on the object of its desire? Surely I am not the type of man to deliver myself over to such exclusivity of objective. So why should she distress herself over these innocuous diversions of mine which in no way involve my affections?' Once had been enough.

But Josephine could not forget how he had loved her, and did not realize that this – as well as a capacity for love that was perhaps lessening as his love of power grew – was precisely what protected her.

Napoleon also liked to think that he came 'into season, like a dog', but judging from the account given by his next mistress, who was a little under sixteen when their affair began, this was certainly not always true. Mlle Georges (Georgina to Napoleon) was an actress, and was playing the apparently unsuitable part of Clytemnestra at the Comédie Française on 28 November 1802 when Napoleon first saw her. When she was invited to St Cloud, she was charmed by 'that enchanting smile which had its equal in no one else', but was not to be easily seduced. The next day, the reaction of her friend and confidant, the great actor Talma (who had known the young Napoleon and even lent him money), was what decided her: 'You hesitate? Are you mad?' he demanded.

Georgina's mind cleared; and from what she recorded next it becomes plain that Napoleon could be a very tender and patient lover indeed, however brutish and short some of his later sexual encounters might have been. She found that he 'overwhelmed me with kindness . . . made himself my *femme de chambre* with so much gaiety, so much grace and tact, that it was impossible not to give in in spite of oneself . . . he made himself humble for my sake.'

But Georgina saw how quickly his moods could change. Now that he was no longer obliged to stifle those rages in which he turned red and white, and which had once seemed to onlookers likely to strangle him, it was others who suffered. On hearing that another admirer (a prince) had given her the

Napoleon was supremely happy at Malmaison

The Battle of Marengo, 1800, meant the end of Austrian power in northern Italy

veil she was wearing, Napoleon tore it from her head and ripped it to shreds. Her cashmere shawl followed. Then he broke her necklace, and finally tore from her finger and ground underfoot a ring which had been a treasured present from her (woman) drama teacher. The next day he tried to make amends by giving her a diamond necklace. Georgina took it all in her young stride.

This was, in fact, one of his most affectionate and light-hearted affairs. On one occasion Georgina was shown into an apparently empty room, and eventually found the First Consul hiding under a huge pile of cushions: when uncovered, he giggled like a schoolboy. He sent for her early one morning so that he could see her 'by daylight', and, when they walked through the woods, bent down to clear all the undergrowth and branches from her path. He saw her at endless performances (this was no hardship since he loved the theatre, and used to say that if Corneille had been living he would have made him a prince) and kept his composure with his mistress on the stage and his wife in the box beside him. One night a bat flew at Georgina, frightening her off the stage, a complete theatrical *faux pas*, but when the bat flew straight on to Josephine she merely laughed and waved it aside with her fan. The two women were utterly different, one sixteen and the other over forty, one high-spirited, frank, independent, reckless, the other sensitive, tactful, gracious, vulnerable. Perhaps Napoleon wanted to sample a little of the teenage fun he had missed by falling in love with a woman who was already in her thirties, and very much a woman of the world, when he met her.

Eugène and Hortense remembered how he had suffered over Josephine's faithlessness, and understood his present need for an occasional change of company; but Josephine was the least philosophical of women, quite unable to rationalize when she herself was suffering the pangs of jealousy, and now she suffered agonies. Only when someone or something that she treasured was threatened did Josephine ever show any courage; and when jealous, as Napoleon himself said, she became a demon.

One of Josephine's ladies-in-waiting now was Hortense's

friend, Claire de Rémusat. (True to her word, Josephine had asked for the Duchess d'Aiguillon to be her first attendant, as she had promised in the Carmes prison, but Napoleon refused on the grounds that she was divorced.) Mme de Rémusat was young but intelligent, and being sure that Napoleon loved Josephine for the peace and solace he found in her company, she tried to calm the jealous wife down. But one morning, at about 1 a.m., she was startled to see Mme Bonaparte rise and say, 'I cannot bear it another minute. Mlle Georges must be up there with him. I am going to surprise them together.' Nothing would dissuade her, so the reluctant Claire followed, carrying a lighted candle. They started up the winding stairs that led to the First Consul's apartments in the Tuileries, when, she recorded,

half way up a noise, muffled but distinct, reached our ears, stopping us in our tracks. Mme Bonaparte turned to me and said 'It must be Roustam, Bonaparte's Mameluke, who guards his door. That devil is capable of slitting both our throats.'

At these words I was seized by such a fright ridiculous as it may now seem – that I waited to hear no more, but went flying down the steps, back to the salon, the candle still in my hand – completely forgetting that I had abandoned Mme Bonaparte in total darkness. She joined me a few minutes later, astonished at my sudden flight. But when she caught sight of my face and the terror written on it she burst out laughing, and I with her, and we renounced our enterprise.

Shortly afterwards, to his wife's great distress, Napoleon announced that from now on he would have a separate bedroom. He later said that Josephine fully realized that a woman's influence over a man sprang primarily from their sexual relationship, and in his own case this was certainly true. But she seems to have regained her calm when she found that he still sometimes wanted to spend the night with her; and she even sometimes became capable, under the constant urging of Eugène, Hortense (who no doubt wished her own husband would be unfaithful and leave her in peace) and Claire de Rémusat, of greater tranquillity during his infidelities. Claire noticed that their occasional arguments did not seem to impair the basic fabric of their relationship at all: 'Indeed,' she wrote, 'it was my observation, the first year I spent at Court, that these rather superficial altercations were invariably followed by reconciliations, and by an ardour and intimacy more pronounced than ever.'

And Napoleon told Roederer, 'If I could not find peace and contentment in my home I should indeed by an unhappy man.'

He must have expressed similar thoughts in a letter to Josephine which he sent from Boulogne, where he was inspecting the men and the fleet with which he was planning to invade England. His letter has been lost, but Josephine replied on 12 November 1803:

> All my sorrows have disappeared in reading the good and touching letter containing the expression of your feeling for me. How grateful I am to you for devoting so much time to your Josephine. If you knew, you would congratulate yourself on being able to bring such joy to the woman you love. A letter is the portrait of the soul and I press this one close to my heart. It does me so much good! I want to keep it for ever. It will be my consolation while you are away, my guide when I am near you, for I want always to remain in your eyes the good, the tender Josephine, solely concerned with your happiness. If a ray of joy touches your heart, if sadness troubles you for an instant, it will be on the breast of your friend that you will spread your happiness and pains; you will have no feeling I do not share. That is my wish and my desire, only to please you and to make you happy . . . Adieu, Bonaparte, I shall not forget the last phrase of your letter. I have kept it in my heart. As if it were engraved there! With what ecstasy my own has replied! Yes, my wish is also to please you, to love you, or rather to adore you.

And though she still called her husband Bonaparte, after nearly eight years of marriage, she now wrote not *vous*, but *tu*. Passion was largely spent. But this new-born unselfishness, like unexpected buds on a wilting plant, would revive the tenderness, the freshness, the innate lyricism of their love.

Librairie Hachette

Napoleon on the terrace at St Cloud
with six of the children in his family.
On his knee is the future Napoleon III
(son of Hortense and Louis), his
nephew and Josephine's grandson

Both Josephine and Napoleon loved
walking in the gardens at Malmaison

Snark Int.

FAMILLE IMPÉRIALE.

MARIE-LOUISE, IMPÉRATRICE.   NAPOLÉON, EMPEREUR.   JOSÉPHINE, IMPÉRATRICE.

NAPOLÉON, DUC DE REICHSTADT.   LA PRINCESSE PAULINE.   JÉRÔME BONAPARTE.   LA PRINCESSE ELISA.

LA REINE CAROLINE.   JOSEPH BONAPARTE.   LA REINE HORTENSE.   LUCIEN BONAPARTE.

LOUIS BONAPARTE.   LAETITIA BONAPARTE.   EUGÈNE BAUHARNAIS.

7. Love, Rouge and Tears

One afternoon Josephine slipped into Napoleon's study un-announced, seated herself on the First Consul's lap, running her fingers gently over his face and through his hair. 'I implore you Bonaparte, do not go making yourself a King,' she said. 'It is Lucien who is urging you to do it: do not listen to him.'

She did not want to see the fortune-teller's prediction that she would be 'more than a Queen of France' come true, for if it did, an heir would surely become still more necessary to Napoleon. If only, she thought, he would allow a Restoration! She was on excellent terms with many royalists; her natural sympathy allied to her upbringing had made her intercede for many returning emigrés, and among them had gained the title of their 'Guardian Angel'. As Claire de Rémusat noted, 'She acted as the original link between the French nobility and the Consular Government.' Napoleon approved this, but he was less pleased when Josephine begged him to accept an offer from the Bourbon pretender, the Count of Provence, who had promised him any position he cared to name – beneath his own of course – in return for being allowed to ascend the throne as Louis XVIII.

Then, in February 1804, a plot to assassinate the First Consul and proclaim the Count of Provence king was discovered: the English had given money to the royalist armies. The secret police set to work, and at the trials that followed twenty-one of the conspirators were condemned to death. Josephine's pleas for clemency were so insistent that nine of them were finally reprieved. Next, to her horror, Napoleon told her that he had ordered a virtual posse to cross the border into Baden to kidnap the Duke of Enghien, the thirty-two-year-old brother of the dead Louis XVI, and the last of the Condé line. He was to be brought to Vincennes for trial. There was only the flimsiest circumstantial evidence against him, yet something in Napoleon's manner convinced Josephine that the prisoner would be condemned to death. She confided in Claire de Rémusat, a staunch royalist, who cried, 'My God, Madame, what will they do to him?' Josephine replied, 'I have done all I could to make Bonaparte promise me that the Prince will not

The Imperial Family—including the two Empresses   123

be sentenced to death, but I am very much afraid that a decision has already been made.'

Napoleon slept with his wife for the next two nights, and each time she argued and pleaded with him. According to Lucien, she even threatened him, saying, 'Think, Bonaparte: if you insist on having your prisoner executed, you may end up like my first husband, on the guillotine, with me beside you.'

But the emotional dependence he usually showed upon her in times of stress no longer ran over into his judgement. The wife who had facilitated 18 Brumaire was not to be allowed to advise on political matters now: public opinion and history were both to judge this decision of Napoleon's a crucial blunder, the throwing away of one of his major assets. As always, Josephine's instincts were right. Finally, having told her that 'women should not interfere in affairs of state', he snapped out an order forbidding her even to mention the subject again.

A curious scene followed that evening. Hortense's child, now eighteen months old, was with them at dinner, and Napoleon played with the child almost raucously, standing him in the middle of the table, and laughing while he overturned the dishes; then he sang through his teeth; next he recited some poetry in a low voice, and finally invited Claire de Rémusat to a game of chess, which she had frequently found him playing over the past two or three days. She looked deathly pale.

When Napoleon demanded to know why she was not wearing rouge, she avoided a direct confrontation with him and merely said that she had forgotten it. He burst out laughing. 'That would never happen to you, Josephine,' he said. 'There are two things that suit women very well: rouge, and tears.' And thereupon, the anguished Claire was amazed to see, he 'approached his wife and began to play with her with more licence than decorum.' Apparently this display was as forced as Claire had felt his gaiety to be, for he spent the night alone, perhaps fearing the last plea that might make him change his mind. At 6 a.m. on 21 March (1804) Enghien was shot, and his body thrown into a grave that had been dug before he was tried.

Napoleon's valet Constant entered his bedroom soon afterwards to find his master depressed and suffering from a headache. A few minutes later Josephine ran in, dishevelled and weeping 'Oh my dear, what have you done?' He replied that the Bourbons must be taught a lesson: they could not 'be allowed to hunt me down like a wild beast', and added gently, and so mistakenly, 'You are a child when it comes to politics'. He would never remove this stain from his name, although years later Josephine would try to excuse it to her ladies-in-waiting, saying that he had been 'wrongly advised'.

But if the nation wanted a crown it should have a crown: his own. At nineteen he had written 'There are very few kings who have not deserved to be dethroned', but now, at thirty-four, he hoped to be among them. On 18 May, less than two months after Enghien's death, the French Senate proclaimed him 'Emperor of the Republic', since he found the grander title more palatable than the simple 'King' favoured by Talleyrand. Carnot (the former Director, a military genius who became Napoleon's Minister of War and then finally Minister of the Interior with the title of Comte) remarked drily: 'You should have remained First Consul. You were the only one in Europe, and look at the company you are in now.'

Napoleon made Joseph and Louis princes, which made Hortense a princess, but Lucien, with whom Napoleon had recently had a serious break, received no title, not did the sisters Caroline and Elisa. (Pauline had remarried in 1803, to the Italian Prince Borghese, and thus had her own title.) Caroline, on hearing Hortense called 'Princess', burst into tears, then fainted. The royal apartments rang with rancour. Finally Napoleon said: 'To hear you, one would think I had robbed you of the inheritance of our father the King!' But he relented, and the sisters became 'Princesses'.

The breach with Lucien was serious: Letizia had gone so far as to take his part and leave with him for Rome. Since his first wife's death, Lucien had been living with a woman whose husband was still alive. At last he died and the two planned to marry, to the infuriated disgust of Napoleon who had chosen the Queen of Etruria as a bride for him. But Lucien would not be dissuaded, and married the woman he had lived with and had a child with. After a stormy midnight conference with Lucien at St Cloud, Napoleon emerged, flung himself into an armchair, and announced to Josephine and the Rémusats (both for once in the same place) that this was the final break with Lucien. Josephine had suffered more from Lucien than from Napoleon's other brothers, but now she tried to defend him.

'What a good woman you are!' said Napoleon, looking at her thoughtfully; then he stood up and took her in his arms, stroking her hair, while he reported all the details of their conversation. The contrast between Josephine's beautiful shining hair, exquisitely arranged, and the dark, sombre face of her husband beside it, made it a striking scene; and Napoleon's next words burnt themselves into the memory of those present. 'It is hard, to find such resistance to such great interests in one's own family. So I must isolate myself from all the world, and rely on myself alone. Well, then, I shall suffice unto myself – and you, Josephine, shall console me for everything.'

Could she console him for his lack of an heir? She thought she had done so, in Hortense's child, whom he loved so much. The title of Emperor was hereditary: but at the suggestion that little Napoleon-Charles should be named his official successor, yet another savage family storm broke out. Louis could be as jealous of rank as he was of Hortense, who, almost broken now in spirit and damaged in health, had one guard standing outside her door and another below her window to keep mythical and real men out. 'What have I done to be disinherited?' he demanded of his brother. Like the other brothers, he probably hoped he might become Napoleon's heir himself; but in any event the thought of his own son taking precedence over him was unbearable – the more so because, as Josephine explained to Claire de Rémusat, 'our enemies pretend the child is Bonaparte's, and that is quite enough to keep Louis from coming to an arrangement with him'. The hideous seed that Lucien had planted in Louis's mind had borne its bitter fruit.

Not satisfied with this, the Bonapartes now redoubled their efforts in the campaign to have Josephine divorced before she could be crowned Empress. Hortense wrote: 'A family conference was called, but the virulence of the Emperor's brothers was so obvious . . . that the Emperor could not fail to

126

see his family's relentless hatred of the Empress.'

In the end it was his sense of justice, still clear on some matters, that came to his aid and allowed him to do as he wanted. In a dissertation on his family, he told Roederer, now his secretary:

My wife is a good wife, who does them no harm. She is content to play the Empress a little, to have diamonds, beautiful clothes, the deserts of her age. I have never loved her blindly. If I make her Empress, it is through justice. I am above all a just man. If I had been thrown into prison, instead of ascending a throne, she would have shared my lot. It is only fair that she should share my elevation. She is always the target of their persecutions . . . Yes, she shall be crowned! She shall be crowned, if it costs me 200,000 men . . .

The Bonapartes' unconcealed hatred had boomeranged and destroyed their own cause. How good, kind, lacking in malice, even ready to turn the other cheek, was Josephine, in comparison with his family of vipers. How childlike, fresh and spontaneous were her emotions and pleasures compared with the worldly greed and pride of his sisters. How affectionate, tender and charming she was in comparison with his mother, who kept her basically kind heart hidden tight under her severe exterior, and who, in spite of her sound basic intelligence, could be dismissed by Laure Permon as 'very ignorant'. How much Josephine *enjoyed* his company, what pleasure she got out of her muslins, her *mousselines de soie,* the beautifully equipped toilet table he had given her, her pretty hair decorations of diamond ears of wheat or golden poppies, intertwined with her own flowers from Malmaison, while his own family saw him only to demand and to argue. How much she loved, but how little she demanded of him for her children. How much he had loved and still did love her, not blindly, as he proudly said, but knowing all her frailties. And how she loved and understood him.

Ten years before he married Josephine, on 3 May 1786, he had confessed: 'My life is a burden because nothing gives me pleasure and everything is painful. It is a burden because the men among whom I live and shall probably always live are as different from me as the moon is from the stars. So I cannot live the kind of life that is bearable and therefore everything is distasteful.' There had been echoes of this sense of isolation through the years until he met Josephine; and since then, only when he feared that she did not love him. She had transformed life for him, given meaning to his ambition, crowned his success with pleasure. She was capable of emotion as deep and intense, if not as sustained, as his own. They shared a capacity for suffering, for depression, for enjoyment, and for love.

Mlle Avrillon, one of Josephine's devoted maids, saw his dependence on her and her swift response to his needs: 'Whenever he suffered the slightest indisposition, when any problem arose to worry him, she was, so to speak, at his feet, and at such times he could not get along without her.'

Méneval, who later replaced Bourrienne when the latter was found in one too many financial rearrangements, saw how he reacted after their altercations, usually caused by her jealousy: 'I have often seen him, after scenes of jealousy caused by Josephine's always anxious affection, so disturbed in mind that he remained for hours, half reclining on the sofa in his study, a prey to silent emotion and unable to resume his work.'

Remorse then struck him; but it was not apparently always entirely unmixed with an element of pleasure at Josephine's reaction, which he evidently took as an involuntary expression of love, since Hortense remembered: 'When the Emperor said with a smile and a satisfied air "My wife was jealous", he seemed pleased about it.' And Claire de Rémusat noticed the greater intimacy and affection that invariably followed.

In the autumn of this crucial year of 1804 came a scene to end them all. Josephine now forty-one, had gone on yet another search for fertility, this time at Aix-la-Chapelle. Napoleon, now thirty-five, joined her unexpectedly from Boulogne, where he had been on another inspection of preparations for his proposed invasion of England, but her initial joy at seeing him sooner than she had hoped was cut short by the interest he showed in one of her readers, Mme de Vaudey. He would not

128

even let Josephine rest on the occasions, more frequent than ever now, when she was afflicted by her terrible migraines, but forced her from her bed to travel and to attend countless receptions in the Rhineland.

In October Josephine returned to Paris to be with Hortense for the birth of her second child, and heard with relief that Mme de Vaudey had been asked to withdraw from court. Her relief was short-lived, for when Napoleon returned to Paris, he wore the preoccupied air that the whole court recognized as the unmistakable sign of an infatuation. Unlike his stage mistresses and other minor indiscretions, the object of his eye this time was a society woman: Constant had even dropped hints of a 'fine lady' to Mlle Georges, who was seeing little of her former lover at this time. Mme du Dûchatel (called by her contemporaries Mme X in this context as her husband, a good and hardworking man thirty years her senior, knew nothing of the liaison) was a well-bred, aquiline-nosed blonde of twenty, intelligent and ambitious, with blue eyes almost as beautiful as Josephine's own.

One morning when a group of the ladies were in Josephine's salon (Napoleon forbade her to entertain men except Eugène to breakfast or in the early morning) she noticed Mme du Dûchatel slip quietly out of the door. Josephine rushed after her in pursuit, up the little staircase which led to Napoleon's secret 'assignation' rooms. Half an hour later she called Claire de Rémusat into her boudoir, and declared, trembling, 'All is lost'. She recounted how she had heard the two voices inside Bonaparte's bedroom, and had rattled the doorknob, crying out that she, Josephine, was there. Finally the door had been opened, and the intrepid Josephine, like the lioness at Malmaison which had just had cubs, attacked with sharp words. Mme du Dûchatel had burst into tears, then Napoleon had recovered himself and advanced on his wife, who had 'barely managed to escape in time to avoid his violence'. At the moment when she was pouring out this lament she still had not done so, for a few minutes later Mme de Rémusat heard the sound of breaking furniture coming from the Emperor's apartments. As he once admitted, 'I am not very gentle when in a passion.'

For once there was still worse to come. Bonaparte had asked

Eugène to come and take his mother away, and told him he wanted a divorce. Claire was sent to enlist Hortense's aid for her mother, but the poor girl, still recovering from her confinement, said 'I cannot intervene in any way. My husband has expressly forbidden it. My mother has been unwise. She will lose a crown, but at least she will have peace and quiet. Believe me, there are women more to be pitied than she.'

But Hortense, who was well aware of Napoleon's many good qualities and his superiority to Louis in love, continued: 'Any chance of a reconciliation . . . lies in the power she exercises over him with her sweet and gentle nature and her tears. It would be fatal for anyone to interfere. The two of them must be left absolutely alone to work it out themselves.'

How wise Hortense was. By the time Claire returned to St Cloud, the emotional storm had blown over, and the reconciliation, as usual, was 'complete'. But a further blow had fallen on Josephine, a result of ambition rather than anger. Napoleon had said that, in view of his new position as Emperor, a divorce was essential to him. 'I lack the courage to make the decision,' he told Josephine – a statement that was more nearly true than perhaps he yet realized. Therefore he asked that she should spare him the ordeal by voluntarily withdrawing. Although clever, this suggestion was no match for Josephine's instinct. Submissive as always, she told him that she would obey him in this as in everything, but that she would not take the initiative. These manoeuvres were the preliminaries in a battle that could not be won: between Napoleon's ambition on the one side, and his love and sense of justice on the other. And Josephine's love was now so long-suffering that, while she probably knew little better than the amazed onlookers why she clung to him so hard, she did so with a tenacity that showed what residual force there was in a soul that had always been criticized for being light, fragile and superficial. Though he did not know it, this was the thread by which Napoleon's happiness now hung. It would never break of itself, but it could be severed.

But Napoleon and Josephine still had some moments of united triumph before them.

The word 'divorce' on Napoleon's own lips for the first time in cold blood had increased the Bonapartes' baying, and they wore a premature and repellent air of victory. Then Napoleon spoke: not in conference, but in command. The Pope was coming from Rome. Josephine was to prepare herself. The Coronation of the Emperor and Empress of France would take place on 2 December 1804: Napoleon and his Josephine were to be crowned together.

On the day before the Coronation, Josephine was in excellent spirits. Her only tears were tears of joy shed after the dress rehearsal. She even asked Napoleon to make the next day a day of grace, and to pardon Lucien – a slightly heavy-handed mercy, perhaps, and it was in fact some time before the family were reconciled, when Letizia (formally 'Madame Mère' by then) was painted into the formal record of the Coronation from which she had been notably absent (in Rome) on the day itself.

Josephine had special cause for happiness: although neither she nor Napoleon was truly religious, she felt, now that the churches were open again and they attended mass, that she would like their former civil ceremony confirmed at a religious ceremony. The secret ceremony took place on 1 December, and Josephine took care to obtain a copy of the marriage certificate from Cardinal Fesch, Napoleon's uncle, who had performed it. This was a new insurance against divorce; and there was even a law, a section of the Civil Code, which said that no woman over forty-five could be divorced on grounds of 'mutual consent'; and if Napoleon finally decided on a divorce, these would be the grounds that he would be most likely to choose – or rather, to impose – since Josephine had been a paragon of a wife since her husband's return from Egypt, and any other grounds could smack of slander as well as expediency. Only three and a half years to safety!

Hundreds sat up all night before the Coronation. Those women who risked getting some sleep rose about 2 a.m. to get their hair dressed. Since everyone had to be in position before 9 a.m., and since no carriages were allowed and the day was foggy, most had a long, cold, dark walk to Notre Dame, and then a long wait for the royal procession, which left the Tuileries at ten o'clock.

131

Just as Napoleon was about to step into his carriage with Josephine, he turned back to Joseph, with an involuntary rags-to-riches reflex. 'Ah, Joseph,' he said, 'If only Father could see us now!' And had he been in a good humour, Joseph, who in one of his rages against his brother had taken to firing shots from a revolver through a full-length portrait of Napoleon, must have agreed.

For Napoleon, who was too stingy to pay for new blinds for Pauline later in the glaring sun of Elba, who had hounded Josephine for her extravagance, who loathed expenditure on women's clothes – 'a quite ruinous expense, and a very bad investment' – and who thought that the craziest form of expenditure was to indulge a passion for building (the bills for redecoration in the rue de la Victoire and at Malmaison!) had quite different ideas when it came to proclaiming his own power and glory. Nothing, now, could be too magnificent: the day cost the Exchequer some 8,500,000 francs.

The glass and gilt coach had been specially made, and on its roof four eagles supported a crown: it alone cost 114,000 francs. In the procession were 140 horses which had been expensively imported from Spain. Josephine wore some 2,000 diamonds in her crown, diadem and belt; Napoleon's crown of laurel leaves, and his orb and sceptre, were, of course, of gold. His costume was designed by Isabey in a sixteenth-century style. It was of red velvet embroidered with gold, and the mantle was strewn with bees – from a distance these resembled the fleur-de-lys, which it was thought unwise to revive at the moment. He also wore a hat which bore a white ostrich feather and diamonds.

Josephine wore white satin, also scattered with golden bees, and with a tiny ruff; her sleeves were long. Her chestnut hair was exquisitely dressed and surmounted by her diadem of pearls and diamond leaves; her complexion, dazzling, had been attended to by Isabey, and she was so happy that she looked, even to the critical eyes of her ladies-in-waiting, about twenty-five; while Mlle Georges, who was smarting from Napoleon's neglect of her, was intoxicated with admiration for the Empress.

After the Pope had crowned Napoleon, the Emperor took it

upon himself to crown Josephine. Laure Permon, who could be very cutting, admitted: 'I have had the honour to be presented to many *real princesses,* to use the phrase of the Faubourg St Germain, but I never saw one who, in my eyes, presented so perfect a personification of elegance and majesty.' Among all the beautiful women present, Josephine stood out for her exquisite figure, her elegant way of holding her head, even the tilt of her neck.

Napoleon's pride was visible in his face as Josephine walked towards him. Then, as she knelt before him, he saw the tears falling on her clasped hands, and 'both he and she appeared to enjoy one of those fleeting moments of pure felicity unique in a lifetime'. He fussed as her *femme de chambre* might have done to balance the crown perfectly on her head.

As she rose, the three Bonaparte sisters let the full weight of the train fall behind her, so that she staggered: Napoleon hissed at them, and they quickly picked it up again, as the *Vivats* rang out.

The coronation procession lasted for five hours, and Josephine's diadem and crown weighed over three pounds, but Napoleon, enchanted by the vision of what he had created, the bride, his Empress, would not let her remove it when they reached the Tuileries. They dined together tête-a-tête in their private apartments, the crown still in position, and Napoleon lavished praises on her.

But the position Napoleon had so wanted had, as he realized, its tremendous drawbacks. A few weeks before he had told Mlle Georges, 'In a position like mine one is loved so little.' After the Coronation his isolation almost inevitably increased, and Bourrienne remarked that now it was 'only through Josephine that the truth was ever to reach the Emperor'.

Five weeks later Mlle Georges received another imperial summons. When she arrived, Napoleon told her, 'Be as you always were, a frank and simple person.' But it was impossible for most people to be like this with him now: his temper was too uncertain, his power too certain. Sadly Georgina reflected, 'The Emperor had driven away my First Consul. Everything was bigger and more imposing now, but there was no space for happiness.'

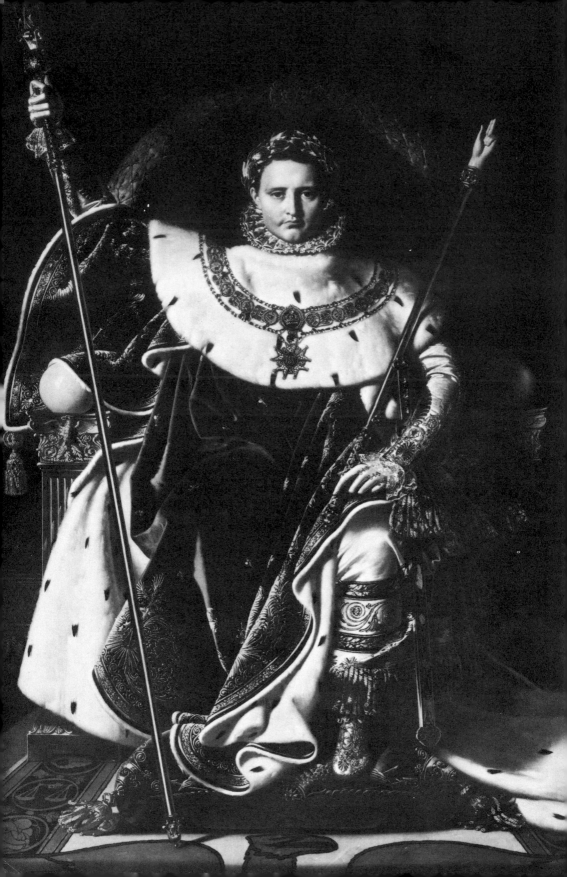

8. A Heavy Crown

Josephine's resistance to her husband's increasing despotism had been sincere and profound. At one point she had told the politician Thibaudeau:

I do not at all approve the schemes that are on foot; I have told Bonaparte so. He listens to me with a great deal of attention, but the flatterers soon make him change his opinion. The new concessions which will be made to him will increase the number of his enemies. The generals are exclaiming that they have not been fighting against the Bourbons in order to exchange their rule for that of the Bonaparte family. I by no means regret having no children from my husband, for I should tremble for their fate. I shall remain attached to Bonaparte's fortunes, whatever perils may attend them, as long as he retains for me the regard and affection which he has always evinced, but the day he changes, I shall retire from the Tuileries.

Thus she pinpointed the course of future events with almost uncanny precision, down to the unhappy life of Napoleon's unborn son, and showed an understanding of political forces far more subtle than Napoleon's own; but she was mistaken about her own willingness to relinquish her husband as soon as he changed. Or, rather, she understood him too well to leave him willingly, realizing as she did, better than anyone else could, how desperately he needed her now, when he shouted at her 'You should submit yourself to all my fantasies. I have the right to answer all your complaints with an eternal I'.

He laid down rules for her conduct as strict as those Alexandre had tried to impose; and now she almost always obeyed. Over the next three years her life became increasingly more grandiose and more narrow as she complied with his exigencies. 'You must not go to the private boxes in the smaller theatres,' he wrote to her during one absence from Court. 'It is not befitting your rank. You should only go to the four big theatres, and always in the Imperial box.' While he was at war, she was to entertain princes and ambassadors as if he were present: but she was to tell them nothing. 'Say nothing,' he told her, 'For whatever you say will be assumed to come from me.'

Extraordinarily, Josephine, who had never bothered with even the faintest hint of discretion as far as her private life was concerned, complied. Admittedly she was increasingly shut out of conferences, and wrote to Eugène saying she knew nothing nowadays of Napoleon's political plans, but it was not necessary to know much in order to say much. Mlle Avrillon said, 'If she tended to be indiscreet about her private affairs, she preserved steadfast silence on public ones.' So she *was* capable of keeping secrets. Thus it seems that she may have released the details of her marriage, which were such common knowledge, almost deliberately, so as to add sympathy to the love she knew the French people already felt for her. Or perhaps it was simply for her own relief that she talked, knowing well that people would gossip about her anyway, and that the truth was infinitely sweeter than others' interpretation of events might be.

An endless stream of people passed through her apartments. Young women, especially, were invited to an early lunch of six or seven courses, usually in the yellow salon, and without even realizing it acquired in Josephine's presence both expertise and polish in the ways of Court. Many suppliants found their way to her rooms, and few, if any, were sent away empty-handed. It was now that Josephine was Empress that Laure Girardin, Alexandre's mistress, sought, and received, her pension. Josephine wrote many letters each day to the Ministries with her recommendations: her spelling was almost as erratic as Napoleon's own, but her grammar was more correct, and her style graceful if not consistently striking.

And everything that she did, everyone she saw, every word she uttered, was reported to Napoleon, who had her watched as closely as he did his mistresses.

Talleyrand, when asked whether Josephine possessed intelligence, replied simply, 'No one ever managed as brilliantly as she without it.' But it was true, perhaps because she had studied books so little in Martinique, and people so closely,

Napoleon loved to see Josephine in white, and she often wore filmy white gowns with a gold border

and perhaps also because of those absurd educational instructions of Alexandre's, that she still found it easiest to learn by talking and watching, easier to absorb information in conversation than to acquire knowledge by reading. Nevertheless once she was interested in a subject, and had made up her mind to master it, she did so with complete thoroughness: she read and knew all about the care of her rare blooms at Malmaison, and commissioned her own exquisite records of them, including the editions of Redouté roses; she gave very precise instructions about the cuttings to be planted by Hortense or her good friends; and she now performed her public duties irreproachably.

She was helped, as Empress, by the Abbé Halna, who bore the title of librarian but in fact was a personal encyclopaedia to whom Josephine could turn for information and help on any subject or any person with whom she was going to deal. So visitors to the new Imperial Court, many of whom must have arrived prepared to enjoy a private laugh at the expense of its crude Corsican and Créole figureheads, were astonished to find that this woman, who had once had the reputation of being a courtesan, had a knowledge of protocol, of their own interests, of the mainsprings of life, and of the details of science and the arts, that forced some of them to award her a higher accolade than they would have accorded a Bourbon princess.

Meeting her could be a great relief after exposure to the Emperor. As Bourrienne had put it, 'Josephine's was the rare talent of putting people at ease, making each person think that he had been singled out for her special welcome...all was gaiety and relaxation in her company. With Bonaparte's entrance, a sudden change came over the room; every eye turned anxiously to read his mood in his expression...he possessed all the qualities for being what society calls "an agreeable man" – all except the wish to be one!' In the growing stuffiness of Court, this was becoming more and more obvious.

The French were paying the price of having in one and the same unpredictable man their Sovereign, and the Head of the Army. Each success on the battlefield brought more adulation at Court, until Napoleon was so fêted that Claire de Rémusat asked herself, 'How was it possible for any human mind not to become somewhat deranged by the excesses of all this praise?' Apparently, it was not entirely possible. The ladies were required to revive or, in the case of the younger ones, to learn the old art of curtseying; and at times the whole Court would be required to file past and bow to an Emperor who had grown bored and furious with the whole idea as soon as he had suggested it, and was now sitting glowering at them.

Nor had his personal courtesy increased. One woman, Mme Regnault, described by Laure Permon as a 'flawless beauty' of twenty-eight, with a Grecian head, raven hair, perfect teeth, and certainly no need of a corset, was approached by her sovereign, who halted in front of her and said loudly, 'Do you know, Mme Regnault, that you are ageing terribly?'

How different from Josephine, who if any of the débutante guests was late (as Laure herself had been on the night of her own presentation at Court) would send someone down to look

*Napoleon's Coronation Coach – now in
the Trianon Museum*

*Napoleon's throne at the summer
Palace of St Cloud. The animal feet
were a typical Empire feature*

One of Josephine's diadems

...bert Josse   *Louvre*

for them, in case they felt too intimidated to come in late and ran home instead!

Yet the man who could be such a bully was still often a coward with women. In the spring of 1805 it was Josephine herself who was asked by Napoleon to break the news to Mme du Dûchatel: he had grown tired of her, or at least of her ambition. 'States are lost as soon as women interfere in public affairs,' he told Roederer. 'The France of the *ancien régime* was ruined by the late Queen.' And he added to Claire de Rémusat that nowadays the French 'would not forgive their sovereign were he to make a parade of his love affairs: they were stricter than they used to be'. If this was true, it was probably because of their affection for Josephine rather than for any more abstract reason.

Josephine as usual complied in this unpleasant task of dismissing the out-moded mistress, who was however allowed to stay at Court, where the Emperor showed her nothing but contempt, and the Empress 'once she saw that she had nothing more to fear', showed no sign that she remembered what had happened – when in fact Napoleon had sought absolution, from her and from his own conscience, by telling her every detail of the affair at Malmaison, as if she had been his confessor. Unquestionably this deepened their mutual understanding, to the amazement of many.

However, Josephine took care that the whole Court should know that her reconciliation with Napoleon was, as always, complete. Constant would enter her bedroom between seven and eight in the morning when he knew that his master had walked the length of the long St Cloud corridor and up the stairs to Josephine the night before. Napoleon would drink some tea, or a tisane of orange leaves, then rise, while Josephine begged him to stay a little longer. 'But I thought you were going back to sleep,' he would laugh and tease, as he tucked the bedclothes back round her, patting her cheek and shoulder, kissing her goodbye.

Later, 'I am late rising this morning,' the Empress would say to her ladies-in-waiting, rubbing her delicate little hands together almost gleefully. 'But then, you see, Bonaparte has

Napoleon crowns Josephine. David later painted Letizia into the picture: in fact she was in Italy at the time

Photo Bulloz

spent the night with me.'

But though her magic remained potent for him, its sphere was now circumscribed. 'My mother had influence over her husband only in unimportant matters,' Hortense said, and both of them had cause to regret this doubly.

In May 1805 Napoleon was crowned King of Italy at Milan, and Josephine Queen beside him; but when they returned to Paris, Eugène was to stay in Milan as Viceroy of Italy. Josephine, who would a thousand times rather have had the company of her family than see them heaped with honours, wept bitterly at the thought of the separation from her son. Napoleon, perhaps a little piqued, said sharply, 'If separation from your children causes you such anguish, can you not imagine how I must feel? The attachment you show for them makes me feel cruelly my own loss in having none.' The tears fell faster.

But there were no losses on the field of battle. In September Josephine accompanied him as far as Strasbourg at the beginning of his campaign against the Austrians and Russians. She was not allowed to go any further with him, and stayed there with a public programme of receptions, plays, balls, and private indulgences in such purchases as new plants for Malmaison and animals for the zoo.

His letters told her briefly of the conditions and the outcome. The weather was terrible, and he told her 'when it rains I change my uniform twice a day'. By late October he had forced the capitulations of the Austrians at Ulm; then, at the beginning of December, came one of his greatest and most terrible battles, against the Russians, the Prussians who had recently joined them, and the remnants of the Austrians, at Austerlitz. Napoleon anticipated exactly the moves that the Coalition armies would make against him, and noted the day before the battle, 'Whilst they march towards my right' (in an attempt to cut him off from Vienna) 'they will expose their flank'. They did: and afterwards 18,600 Russian bodies were counted on the field, against 900 French. He immediately wrote to Josephine, 'I have beaten the Russian and Austrian armies commanded by the two Emperors. I am somewhat tired, as I have bivouacked in the open for a week, on nights that are fairly cold.

Tonight I sleep in the chateau. . . . The Russian army is not just beaten, it is destroyed. I kiss you.' Two days later he wrote giving her more details of the price of victory, the numbers of dead and wounded, and admitted 'what a horrible sight!'

The Czar Alexander was in tears of despair; the Austrians lost the last of their Italian lands and the Tyrol, and until a new and more powerful Coalition was formed Napoleon was more than ever before the master of Europe. On 30 December he rejoined Josephine at Munich.

But before long there was to be another blow to family unity. She had found great joy, recently, in the company of Hortense and her two little grandsons, and had been able to devote herself to them more wholeheartedly since she had been less tormented by her own emotions. Hortense had written to Eugène in Milan telling him, 'Maman is behaving very well. She no longer makes jealous scenes, which is a great improvement.'

But now Napoleon decided to put Louis on the throne of Holland, which meant that Josephine would be separated from her daughter as well as her son. It is hard to say which of the two women grieved most. For Hortense, it was the snapping of the last link with normality: from now on, she felt, there would be no respite, however brief, from Louis's brooding jealousy. She described the move as 'the cruellest ordeal of all those destiny had in store for me'.

Josephine was distressed by her knowledge of this as well as by her own sense of loss. She wrote to Eugène, 'I am completely laid low by your sister's departure. I experienced the same anguish as I felt when you went away. I have been too upset and too ill to write to you sooner.'

'Now Bonaparte, don't go making yourself a king,' she had said. How right she had been.

Meanwhile she had often been deprived of Napoleon's company too, though on occasion her pleas to be allowed to accompany him on his journeys had been granted – on condition, her little Mlle Avrillon noted scathingly (she hated the *unreasonable* demands made on her mistress), that she *promised* not to suffer from her migraines.

After the celebrations of Austerlitz, 1806 had started well.

In January, Eugène married the eighteen-year-old Bavarian Princess Augusta, a pretty girl with whom this good-hearted, charming and amusing young man was blissfully happy. Hortense was forbidden by Louis to join the rest of the family for the wedding, and wrote despairingly to Josephine instead. By now she lacked not only the will, but probably even the physical strength, to withstand him. The Murats, however, were ordered to attend the ceremony, and were so furious on hearing that Napoleon was also adopting Eugène as his son, that Murat broke his sword.

These two were now the spearhead of the Bonapartes' continuing campaign against Josephine. In the end Napoleon was to feel more bitter about their betrayal – particularly his sister's – than perhaps any other; even early on he divined that they were capable of almost any crime that would further their ambition, and once said to the little Napoleon-Charles, within Caroline's hearing, 'If you value your life, my poor child, I advise you not to dine with your cousins.'

The Murats had introduced Mme du Dûchatel to Napoleon. Mlle Georges records that when her own liaison with the Emperor was fading out, Murat took her for a drive in his carriage and tried to persuade her to persist: Napoleon, he assured her, was still very fond of her. And now the Murats presented the Emperor with Eléonore Dénuelle de la Plaigne who, like Caroline and Hortense, had been to Mme Campan's school. She was a tall graceful brunette, with exceptionally dark eyes, eighteen years old, and only two months married to a man who had then been arrested on a charge of forgery. By September (1806) she was several months pregnant by her lover.

And it was in September that Napoleon set out for the Rhineland, from where he was to attack the great new coalition of Prussia, Russia, Saxony and England. He never resumed the affair with Eléonore.

The original plan had been for Napoleon to set out for the Rhineland alone, and for Josephine to follow, more slowly, to join him at Mainz. But Josephine dreaded their separation more than ever these days, with the rest of her own family far away, and his still laying their endless snares. She persuaded him to take her with him, and they set out from St Cloud together.

For once it was M. de Rémusat who was in attendance, and his observation was as keen, if less interpretative, than Claire's usually was. When Napoleon had to leave Josephine after three days together in Mainz, he held her for a long time in his arms, 'as if unwilling to release her'. Talleyrand was also present (and not yet in disfavour). Still holding Josephine, and holding out a hand to his Minister, the Emperor said twice 'It is hard indeed to leave those one loves best in the world'.

Then he burst into tears which, to the consternation of all, were followed by a spasm: 'he went into convulsions which brought on severe vomiting.' Josephine and some of his close staff had once witnessed a similar fit when one of his mistresses – probably Mlle Georges – was with him and, terrified, summoned help by ringing the bell-rope. Her fears about her husband were not now simply about his fidelity, but about his health, both physical and mental. She had always feared, as she had put it in her letter wondering whether to marry, whether his ambition might not push him too far.

Her own anxieties were not alleviated by the tactlessness of Mme de la Rochefoucauld, who let it be known that she did not think Napoleon could beat the Prussians. It was Mme de la Rochefoucauld who had once before reduced Josephine to tears by telling her that she did not insist on sufficient discipline among her ladies: now she was imposing on this very good nature herself. Napoleon heard of the incident, and was furious. 'You should make it clear that you are offended, and forbid her to say things in your salon which might reach the general public and create a bad impression. Your mistake is being too nice to people who do not deserve it . . .'

A round of official duties and entertainments, a never-ending series of galas, fêtes, pageants, plays and fireworks, did nothing to cheer Josephine, although as usual her hosts would never have guessed this. There was some respite however: Hortense was actually allowed to visit her, and brought her two sons with her. But however she had spent the evening, night after night, when she got home, Josephine got out her packs of cards and tried to tell: would it be victory or defeat?

Three weeks after Napoleon had left, she cried jubilantly to her ladies-in-waiting that a great victory was imminent. Within minutes, the doors were thrown open and a pageboy, caked in mud from his journey, knelt to hand her a letter: the Prussians and Mme de la Rochefoucauld had lost.

But Napoleon did not send for her, and Josephine cried. He sent letters: 'Talleyrand has arrived and tells me that you do nothing but weep. But why? You have your daughter, your grand-children, and good news . . .'

In another letter replying to an angry one of hers (he had recently written scathingly about some of the queens he was meeting and their interference in affairs of state) he said: 'It is true that I hate intriguing women above all else. I am used to women who are good, gentle and conciliatory; those are the sort I like . . . it's not my fault, but yours . . . I like only women who are good, simple and sweet, because only such women are like you.'

The Russians were now in flight, and he crossed into Poland, where at the beginning of December he wrote simply and plaintively 'the nights are long here, alone'. But he made no move to allow her to come. Perhaps he knew as well as she the damage that distance might do to them: and desired it, as he was still incapable of *voluntarily* rejecting her. She wrote again asking to join him. He said that she must stop worrying, that she could join him as soon as winter quarters had been prepared. Meanwhile he relayed the most depressing picture possible of their conditions: camping in a farmhouse, in perpetual rain, with mud up to their knees. It was enough to deter any normal Empress from wanting to join her husband at the front line, let alone one who so loved comfort and her own elegant surroundings; but Josephine did not waver. Within two days, Napoleon had two experiences that began to change his emotional dependence on Josephine.

Her pleas were in vain. He said she must wait 'a few more days': too many. The last day of 1806 was also the last day of this, the ripest and sweetest part of their relationship, which had produced more exotic and compelling fruit than had seemed possible from its bitter-sweet beginnings.

146

Marie Walewska: Napoleon told Lucien "her soul was as lovely as her face"

On 31 December Napoleon received a letter from Caroline Murat. The Emperor and Eléonore had a son. On New Year's Day 1807 the thirty-seven-year-old soldier, thrilled as always to be near the arena of war, changed horses at Bronie and saw a girl waiting to be presented to him on the road to Warsaw.

She welcomed him to Poland, which, like all patriots, she hoped Napoleon might make into an independent buffer state against its, and his, Russian, Prussian and Austrian enemies. A black fur bonnet framed blonde hair and a lovely, gentle face. Her name was Marie Walewska.

On 3 January (1807) Napoleon wrote again to Josephine: 'Your grief touches me; but one must submit to circumstances. There is too much ground to cover between Mainz and Warsaw . . . I rather think that you should return to Paris where you are needed.'

His next letter said, 'Go to the Tuileries, and live the same life that you lead when I am there, that is my wish.'

On 8 January, he wrote, 'Your stay at Mainz is too sad; Paris wants you back; go there, it is my desire. I am more put out than you, for I should have loved to share the long nights of this season with you . . .'

Josephine's reaction was predictable, and Napoleon wrote: 'They tell me that you cry all the time . . . Why these tears and grief? Have you therefore no courage?' and later, 'I am well and I love you very much, but if you go on crying all the time I shall think are without courage and without character; I don't like cowards; an Empress should have courage!'

Meanwhile General Duroc had been finding out all he could about the young girl who had greeted Napoleon by the road. She was nineteen, and she was a Countess, married to a man of seventy. News of the Emperor's interest in her was quick to reach the ears of other Polish patriots, and when Marie, who was tender, strong-willed, shy and religious, the very opposite of a lover of society, refused an invitation to a ball being given for the Emperor on 18 January, pressure from friends and politicians persuaded her to change her mind.

She attended the ball, in a simple white dress of tulle over satin, wearing no jewels. She scarcely danced, although she did have one contra-dance with Napoleon.

Napoleon's effect on the majority of women by this time bore absolutely no relation to his physical or mental charms. The mere presence of the Emperor who had already conquered most of Europe, and seemed about to yoke the rest, was sufficient in itself: he hypnotized and thrilled them with his name alone. The Countess Pococka, who met him on this visit to Warsaw, admitted, 'I was, as it were, stupefied . . . it seemed to me as if there were a halo around his head.'

It was with his usual arrogance, therefore, and without any real attempt to charm, that Napoleon spoke to Marie Walewska. He told her bluntly something he had no doubt learned from Josephine: that white tulle did not look good on white satin.

After the ball she received a note: 'I saw only you, I admired only you, I desire only you. A prompt reply to calm the impatient ardour of N.'

But no such reply came from the Countess Walewska, and

shortly Napoleon was reduced to writing: 'There are moments when fame palls, weighs heavily on the spirit, and it is from this I suffer now.' What good was it to be Emperor if one young girl could cast him into a personal abyss? For a moment he was back in the mood of his twenties, when he had implored Josephine to understand his love, and had been sure that he won battles only in order to win her more completely. For a moment, now, it seemed again that personal might replace political values: but by now the two were so closely intertwined in Napoleon, under the need for absolute power, that there could surely only be one end: affection must now yield to the need to dominate completely.

Even so it was true that for the first time since he had met Josephine, Napoleon was in love – in love in the way that he might have been had he met his wife at the age Marie was now, without the adulatory intoxication Josephine had wrought in his senses, but with a fierce and tender yearning. As for Marie, the three foundation stones of her life were her religion, her country, and her marriage: she was already a mother. From afar, she had admired the idea of this potential saviour for Poland, but she later admitted, 'Close up, the man terrified me. That extraordinary man! He was like a volcano. The passion that ruled him was ambition, but those of love were nevertheless violent, even though they were transitory.'

While Marie lacked the intense and flamboyant quality of Josephine's emotional life and her capacity for supreme enjoyment and sorrow, she possessed many of the other qualities Napoleon so loved in his wife: she was gentle, vulnerable, easily frightened, sweet; if not child-like, she was little more than a child and she was naïve.

Unfairly, therefore, he added his half-promises to the lectures being given to the recalcitrant girl by her countrymen, and wrote, 'Come! All your desires shall be fulfilled. Your country will be dearer to me when you have taken pity on my poor heart.' His style in the flesh was different: menacing, threatening what he would do if she resisted him further, with the fury that could terrify an enemy. She remembered that at his 'savage look' she fainted; he remembered that 'she did not struggle overmuch'. And afterwards, although there was no reward for Poland, he told Lucien that 'her soul was as lovely as her face'. Five days had elapsed since the ball and the only woman who had challenged him for years had been conquered.

For once, however, Napoleon did not resent or struggle against the hold his mistress had over him, as he had so often done in the past. Perhaps the geographical distance from Josephine made his happiness seem entirely deserved, and not at her expense, just as she perhaps had once thought that he could not be hurt in Italy by her friendship with Hippolyte Charles in Paris. The fact that Marie, while ambitious for her country, entirely lacked personal ambition, meant that his affection was unstrained: he trusted her, and knew that he dominated her. She could not be regarded as a threat, so she became a haven to turn to after the battle plans and charts and maps. Unlike most of his affairs, this one was not to end in anger or bitterness, but was gently to flourish in its own quiet and intermittent way, and to give him a peace and satisfaction he had never before found far from Josephine. Thus the mist was beginning to clear from Napoleon's emotional landscape, and though this new territory would finally lack the romantic beauty of the old, it held enough dramatic landmarks to give him confidence. He was no longer dependent on Josephine; *away from her*, he could beget a child by another woman; and *away from her* he could fall in love with another woman.

He never, as Josephine had done, failed completely to write when his heart was elsewhere, but he did become less than his usually hope-sustaining self when he wrote now: 'I had a good laugh over the letter saying that you had taken a husband in order to be with him. I had thought, in my ignorance, that the wife was made for the husband, and the husband for country, family and glory.' He was reverting to overt male Corsican values.

In February, after the battle of Eylau, where both sides suffered terrible losses but the Russians finally withdrew, he sent her 'only two lines tonight, in my fatigue, to tell you that I am well and that I love you'.

Not far from the battle, in East Prussia, stood the Chateau

of Finckenstein, and it was here that Napoleon established his headquarters and waited for a thaw before he returned to the attack. He wrote to Josephine in April: 'there are many fireplaces, which is very pleasant as I rise often during the night. I love to see a fire.' Here he could indulge in his favourite combination, making love and war: for when he rose in the night to study charts and positions, the firelight flickered also on Marie Walewska. She had joined him for an early spring idyll, that would last two months, cut off from the outside world.

He had taken immense precautions to keep Marie's presence secret. His little camp bed had as usual been set up beside the immense fourposter, which he did not use. Marie worked at her embroidery, quietly, in a separate room, while he saw any visitors. Berthier glimpsed her once as she was leaving breakfast. Constant, who served meals, judged her unselfish and charming. She was a strong-minded yet malleable girl, and she suited Napoleon's desire now for complete dominance. His passion no longer terrified her. She would always show him loyalty, and even visited him when he was exiled to Elba. 'He is my all, my future and my life,' she said. Thus, even though Napoleon now lacked the capacity to give himself up completely to the emotion as he had once done, and would certainly safeguard himself from such suffering as he had felt when separated from Josephine, there was genuine love and a genuine desire to please and understand on both sides. It was the first time Josephine had had a flesh and blood rival: previously only Napoleon's imagination could conceive a being who might in some ways equal or surpass her. And although the secret was so closely kept, an Emperor's life was considered public property.

The news winged its way to Josephine in Paris, and she was thrown into a state of extreme agitation and depression. Napoleon replied to one fear – 'Whatever makes you think you are going to die?' and he insisted, in May, 'I love only my little Josephine, who is sweet, sulky and capricious, who does everything – even quarrel – with grace. For she is always amiable, except when she is jealous – and then she becomes a

151

female demon.'

It was not Josephine who died in May, but little Napoleon-Charles, her eldest grandson, now four and a half. He had had a sudden attack of croup. Hortense suffered what sounds like an hysterical paralysis, sitting for hours with her arms linked through the arms of her chair, till one of her frantic staff had the idea of confronting her once more with the tiny corpse, and at last the desperate tears were released. But Hortense, who had now suffered so terribly, said, although her younger son was with her, 'I do not want to love anything on this earth again'.

Even Louis was so concerned at her condition that he personally asked Josephine to come to Laeken, near Brussels, where he proposed taking Hortense. Josephine, herself ill with fever and migraine (the doctors were applying blisters to the back of her neck at St Cloud), had herself reached such a low state that she felt as fearful of Napoleon as Hortense had been of Louis, and dared not leave Paris without permission. The Arch-Chancellor, Cambacérès, always sympathetic to Josephine, called a Council of State which gave her the necessary mandate. There was little she could do for her daughter, who remained shocked for weeks, but at least Josephine was capable of understanding such grief. Even Louis was shattered by the sight of the state Hortense had been reduced to, by the process of his own attrition and this terrible last blow; and a brief reconciliation meant another pregnancy. It was this child, Hortense's third son, who was eventually to become the Emperor's namesake and successor, as Napoleon III.

Napoleon wrote with a mixture of sternness, tenderness, and philosophy to both women. To Josephine: 'I wish I could be near you, so that you could be moderate and understanding in your grief. You are lucky never to have lost a child; but this is one of the conditions and penalties that goes with our human misery. If only I could hear that you had become sensible, and that you are well.' (Letizia had lost four children in infancy.)

To Hortense he wrote: 'My daughter, all that I hear from the Hague tells me that you are not being sensible; however great your grief, it must have limits. Do not injure your health; find some distractions, and realize that life is full of so many dangers, brings so many misfortunes, that death is not the greatest of them.'

Rough words of comfort from a soldier used to seeing people in such agonies on the battlefield that they longed for death, used later to seeing those blinded and crippled in battle, who perhaps wished that they had not survived: but not the words to comfort a desolate young mother to whom life had shown too may forms of cruelty.

But Napoleon, as well as grieving for his grandson, his favourite, was concerned again with the lack of an heir he had fathered himself. After two months with Marie Walewska, who was in her most fertile years, there was no sign of a pregnancy. And there were rumours that little Leon, Eléonore's son, might have been fathered by Murat. Would he ever have a son and heir himself?

At the end of May he left Marie to rejoin his forces, and in mid-June the Russians were soundly defeated at Friedland. Josephine responded to the news with less than her usual tact, for in July he wrote, 'I am hurt to see that you are completely egotistical, and seem uninterested in my military success.'

At Tilsit, on 25 June 1807, Napoleon began what must have been two of the most extraordinary and gratifying weeks of his life. He had invited the Czar Alexander to meet him and to discuss the future of Europe. A tented raft was moored in the middle of the River Niemen, and the two great men were rowed out to it simultaneously from the two banks. Their first meeting (during which they embraced) lasted only half an hour, but it was repeated the following day, after which Alexander moved on to Napoleon's bank and took up residence in the same street. From then on they met every day, studying the map of Europe and planning two mutually exclusive but friendly empires, which might even challenge the naval and commercial power of Britain. Napoleon dictated crushing terms to Frederick William III of Prussia, who was not even invited to observe the proceedings, but of Alexander Napoleon wrote to Josephine, 'I like him very much: he is young, friendly and very good looking, and he has more intelligence than is commonly supposed.' Two years later his enthusiasm for the Czar would be still greater; and five years later, France and Russia would once more find themselves at war with each other. But for the moment peace and Napoleon's good humour were restored, and he wrote to Josephine from Dresden, half way home, 'I shall be extremely happy to see you again. One of these fine nights, very soon, I shall come bursting into St Cloud like a jealous husband . . .' How thankful he was that that was no longer true, that if not really free from love for Josephine he was at least free from the torments that had accompanied his early passion for her, until she had learned to fear her own independence of him, and to submit completely to his will.

Nowadays, even in everyday matters, Napoleon demanded strict obedience. From Finckenstein he had written telling her exactly how grandly she was to live: 'An Empress cannot live like a private citizen.' At the time of the Coronation she had had seventeen ladies-in-waiting, but this number had risen to thirty in 1807. And, as Josephine would later admit, the increasing ceremony and ritual bored and tired her. So it did others. Claire de Rémusat said: 'the larger the court, the stricter the ceremonial and the more impersonal and monotonous the life had become; and as the Emperor's despotism increased, so did the fear and silence among the courtiers. All former intimacies with him ceased . . . His wife came gradually to the same state of dependency as the rest – shut out, like all the rest.'

When he returned to St Cloud at the end of July (1807), there must have been many as apprehensive as Josephine herself. Napoleon was in a good mood, and as usual he dined tête-à-tête with his wife. But she had lost almost all confidence in herself and her situation, which seemed as uncertain as the hour at which the Emperor might deign to appear for dinner: some nights the cooks roasted chicken after chicken after chicken, until at last he was ready to stop working and eat his usual small portion: it might be the thirtieth or the fiftieth chicken that provided the Emperor's dinner.

In August Jerome Bonaparte was married, and Josephine found her first new (possibly because unafraid) admirer for some time: Frederick Louis, the Crown Prince of Mecklenburg-Schwerin, who was still in his twenties, good looking, and reasonably intelligent, if not quite aware of Napoleon's psychology.

The young man stayed on after the wedding celebrations to work on details of the Confederation of the Rhine, to which the German principalities were to be admitted. Claire noticed that while the Prince was clearly romantically interested in Josephine, she was making such an effort not to play the coquette – in the delicious manner that was as natural to her as breathing – that she did not appear quite herself, but was 'trembling lest she displease her husband'. Privately, however, she was pleased enough at Frederick's admiration to laugh when people mentioned it.

More plots in the Bonapartes' conspiracy against her had now come to her ears, and she wrote to Eugène at the beginning of September (1807) telling him of the Murats' latest attempt to get the Emperor to divorce her. (Napoleon's immediate research on returning to Paris had been about the paternity of Leon: however his interrogation of Eléonore, and the child's looks, had convinced him that though Murat had certainly been the girl's lover too, the child was his own.) She told Eugène: 'Unfortunately, the Emperor is so great that no one dares tell him the truth any more; he is surrounded by flatterers from morning to night. As for myself, you know that I only want one thing: his love. If they should succeed in separating me from him, it is not the loss of rank I should regret.'

She also told Eugène that she was making no more jealous scenes: in fact, she later took the part of his present mistress, Mlle Grassini, yet another of the readers to succumb to her mistress's husband, and refused to allow Napoleon to dismiss her. Another personal grief had been added to her distress. Her mother had died in June at Trois-Ilets, having become more or less a recluse in spite of the pension Josephine had obtained for her, and having refused to make the journey to live in state in France. Napoleon had withheld the news for a while till Josephine had recovered a little from the shock of her grandson's death.

Eugène replied that talk of a possible divorce was heard in Munich as well as in Paris; but, with that exemplary fairness of his, he said: 'If his Majesty continues to harass you about the necessity of having children, tell him that it is not just for him to persist in reproaching you on that point. If he believes that his own happiness, and that of France, depends on his having heirs, then he must act accordingly. He must treat you well, give you sufficient funds and allow you to live with your children in Italy . . . We shall remain no less attached to him.' As usual, the Beauharnais were as united as the Bonapartes were divided.

Then one Sunday before mass Fouché asked to speak to her, and to her contempt and horror suggested that she should withdraw for 'the national good'. She already knew that Fouché had said how convenient her death would be: a remark that caused Napoleon to tell Lucien later that Josephine 'cries every time she has indigestion, believing she has been poisoned by those who want me to re-marry'. Hardly surprising! However, Josephine's sense of dignity and justice was outraged by the crudity of Fouché's suggestion, and Napoleon (who may already have known about it, but could never withstand the honesty of Josephine's heart) reprimanded him sternly.

He told Talleyrand: 'Were I to divorce my wife, I would be giving up all the charm she has brought to my private life. I would have to start all over again to learn and to accommodate myself to the tastes and habits of a new and possibly very young wife. This one adjusts herself to mine and understands me perfectly. Then, too, I would be displaying ingratitude for all she has done for me. I am not actually beloved by my people. Divorce from a beloved Empress would not enhance my popularity . . .' Even he had noticed that the roll-call of victories no longer had its previous power, that at Court 'I arrange all the entertainment, yet everyone seems tired and sad'. Without Josephine, for him and for them, it would be unbearable.

In November he went to Italy, and for once Josephine, who could bear pressure but not tension, was so pleased to have the source of her uncertainties taken away that she did not seek to accompany him. He made Eugène now his successor to the throne of Italy: *if* he had no male heirs of his own.

In Italy Lucien was again the cause of one of those famous rages, which were becoming still more frequent. His brother still refused to leave his wife in return for any power or honours Napoleon offered him. The Emperor threw his watch on the floor and screamed, 'Since you won't listen to reason, I will break you as I break this watch.'

He now had designs on Spain, and his armies were taking up their positions for the Peninsular War. Hearing this on his return to Paris, Josephine asked would he never be satisfied: 'Will you never stop making war?' 'Do you think I enjoy it?' he retorted, apparently unaware of the truth that was by now quite obvious to everyone else, in his own Court as well as throughout most of Europe.

The year 1808 opened ominously for Josephine. While Napoleon had been in Italy she had gone to the theatre, and not one of the four permitted grand ones, in a party including Prince Frederick. She had been dressed incognito, and sat in a private grilled box. But Napoleon was furious: Josephine received a punishing letter, and the Prince received his notice, two days to quit France. Now, on tenterhooks lest she should make the merest slip, she wrote to Eugène, expressing openly her hope in the line of conduct that she had pursued, more or less perseveringly, ever since Bonaparte's return from Egypt in 1799: 'My only defence is to live in such a way as to leave myself open to no reproach.' But now it must be taken to extremes: 'I no longer go out, I have no pleasures . . . Oh! My dear Eugène, what an unhappy seat a throne makes! I would renounce my own and those of my children tomorrow and without a pang. The Emperor's heart is all I care about. Should I lose it, I would care little for all the rest.'

Then one morning in the spring of 1808 Talleyrand was summoned to the Emperor. When he emerged from his study he had news that saddened Claire de Rémusat. His Majesty had reached a final decision: he was definite, he wanted a divorce.

9. The Sacrifice

A play was to be performed that night at the Tuileries. Those who had already heard the news that Napoleon wanted a divorce must have wondered how Josephine would look when she arrived, if she arrived. Princes and ambassadors and courtiers waited, and waited. Long after the performance should have begun word came that it should take place without Their Majesties: the Emperor was slightly indisposed.

Immediately after the play, Talleyrand and M. de Rémusat went to inquire after Napoleon's health. They were told that at 8 p.m. he had closed and bolted his doors and retired to bed – with Josephine.

'What a devil of a man!' exclaimed Talleyrand, 'continually giving way to his first impulse, unable to decide what he wants to do. Let him make up his mind, so that we may know what position to take with him on this issue.'

For once Talleyrand's thoughts had not been so very dissimilar from Josephine's own. She and Napoleon had eaten dinner in cold silence, and she had then retired to her boudoir to dress for the performance. Suddenly a messenger asked her to go to the Emperor, and she found him in a severe state of nerves, and suffering from painful spasms of the stomach. She was not long left in doubt as to whether this was his usual indigestion, or brought on by more serious causes.

At the sight of her he burst into tears. She was already fully and elegantly dressed, but disregarding this he pulled her down on the bed beside him, repeating over and over again, 'My poor Josephine, I shall never be able to leave you.'

With considerable strength of mind, considering how she had been dreading this moment of decision, Josephine replied: 'Sir, calm yourself, make up your mind what you want to do and let us put an end to these devastating scenes.'

Had he been capable of doing just that, they might both have suffered less. But her resolution seemed to agitate him still more violently. His condition became so acute that she begged him to cancel going to the play, and go to bed instead.

M. de Rémusat recorded Josephine's own version of what

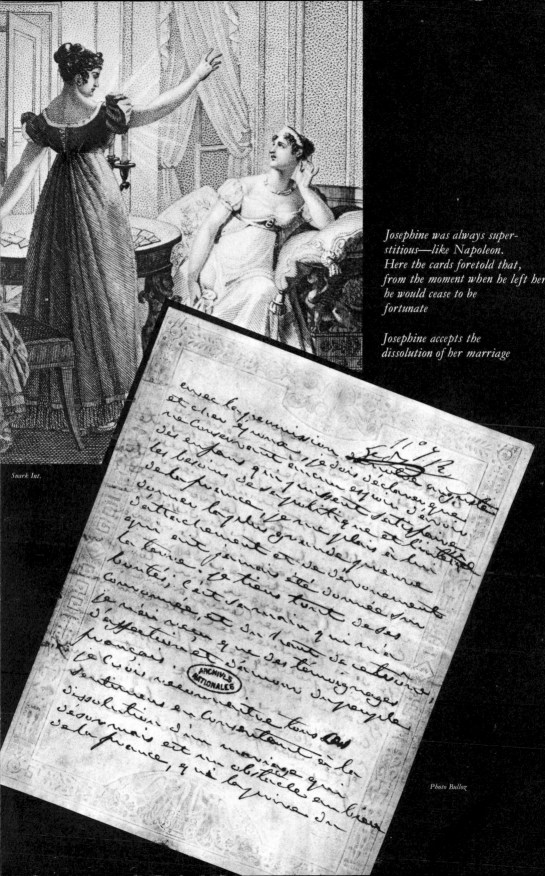

Snark Int.

Josephine was always superstitious—like Napoleon.
Here the cards foretold that,
from the moment when he left her
he would cease to be
fortunate

Josephine accepts the
dissolution of her marriage

Photo Bulloz

happened next: 'To win his consent, nothing would do but that she must, that very instant, step out of her elaborate attire and share his bed, which, as the Empress said, he literally soaked with his tears, repeating over and over again, "I am surrounded by people who torment me and make my life a hell."

'It was a night of tender love interspersed with intervals of restless sleep.'

M. de Rémusat continued with his own summary of events: 'Later the Emperor regained control of himself, and he was never again to betray such turbulent emotion. Thus it was that the Empress vacillated between hope and fear. She did not entirely trust these pathetic scenes . . . She thought that what he wanted was, by constant torment, to disgust her with him, to exhaust her strength and patience, and to bring her to a state of collapse – or perhaps something even worse . . .'

Josephine's subjective interpretation is very understandable, and reveals how her own love was being eroded by this appalling uncertainty; but if she had been right Napoleon would certainly have chosen this moment to make the final decision, as she asked him to. In fact he knew in his heart that he was spiritually and emotionally, and to a great extent also physically, hers and hers alone: the young idealistic Corsican had found his dream at the moment when confirmation of his manhood had been crucial, and he could not now reject it at will. In her presence, this knowledge became a blinding and exquisite truth that eclipsed all reason.

When he himself finally realized this, Napoleon would take endless trouble to avoid being left alone with the only woman in the world who for him remained irresistible.

But for the moment his attention was once more seized by events in Spain.

He saw his chance for seizing Spain when civil war broke out following the unwilling abdication of Charles IV in favour of his son, Ferdinand VII. The royal parties were summoned to a conference with Napoleon at Bayonne, where the Emperor relieved them of their problems by putting his brother Joseph on the throne instead. Caroline and Joachim Murat were now allocated Joseph's old position, and became King and Queen

Joseph Bonaparte, Napoleon's elder brother, was always in his shadow. He was created King of Spain but ran away when war broke out

of Naples, and more rapacious than ever.

Josephine accompanied Napoleon on this trip, which lasted nearly three months. Their guests were tedious and harder to deal with socially than politically, so the Emperor and Empress took every chance of enjoying themselves together, and alone. Away from the protocol of Court they drove with delicious abandon along the Bay of Biscay, even stopping for the almost unheard of pleasure of exploring the empty beaches, and running hand in hand to race the tide. Then came a three week journey back to the capital, by way of towns in the South and West that Napoleon, so busy always with Austria, Italy,

161

the Rhineland, Poland, and Russia, had never seen. Days were spent at receptions, luncheons, civic balls and fêtes, nights jolting over the rough roads. Josephine's migraine returned, but she managed to bear up until they reached St Cloud, where she almost collapsed. A few weeks later Napoleon left to meet the Czar once more, this time at Erfurt.

These six months, from April to September, had been among the happiest Josephine could remember, and she wrote to Eugène: 'You know how many discomforts I have endured: my head has felt them . . . I have suffered horribly. The Emperor has shown his affection for me by his concern: he has been getting up as many as four times a night to come and see me. For the past six months he has been nothing less than perfect towards me.'

She saw him for ten days on his return from Germany, then he left Paris for a second trip to Spain. This time he refused to allow Josephine to go with him. He had been sleeping badly. One night in Germany Constant had rushed in to his bedroom, hearing dreadful groans, and had found him in a terrible state after a nightmare in which, he said, 'A bear seemed to be tearing out my vitals'. A Russian bear? Josephine was becoming desperately afraid that he would be assassinated, and instructed Constant to keep yet closer watch.

On 9 January 1809, Napoleon wrote to her: 'I see from your letter that you have dark forebodings. Austria will not make war on me.' But Austria was planning to do that, and so was Russia, both with the connivance of Talleyrand and Fouché, and the collusion of the Murats: Caroline cared little for her brother's fate if she could replace him with her husband.

He returned to Paris two weeks later. Talleyrand and Fouché were rebuked in public, before a council of state, and Talleyrand removed from his office of Grand Chamberlain, but they were not eliminated from all service: this was an instance where he could well have afforded to be more ruthless. Talleyrand had earlier been replaced as Minister of Foreign Affairs by Champagny, and to this man Napoleon admitted once more his emotional dependence on Josephine: 'If I had the misfortune to lose her, reasons of state would force me to marry again, but I should only be marrying a womb. She alone should have been my companion for life.'

News that the Austrians had crossed the River Inn and taken Munich reached Napoleon at the Elysée on 12 April (1809). 'This means war,' he said. It would be his fourth war against the Austrians. Immediately and in secret preparations were made for his departure, and in the early hours his carriage was made ready. When he went down to it at 4.15 a.m., Josephine, who had heard of his imminent departure, ran downstairs after him in the first clothes she had been able to seize, without stockings, and with only thin slippers on her feet. Constant said she was 'crying like a child'. At the sight of her, Napoleon, who had wanted to leave unencumbered by her baggage and her staff, relented: he threw a pelisse over her to keep her warm, and ordered that her luggage should be sent after her. So they drove off together in the darkness on what was to be their last journey together.

He left her in Strasbourg while he pushed on to the Rhine. Within three weeks he had taken Vienna, and was advancing still. Josephine went to Plombières with Hortense and her children for June and July, and returned to Malmaison in August.

It was here that she learned in the autumn that Marie Walewska was at last pregnant. Napoleon had summoned her to join him at Schönbrunn during the Austrian campaign, and they had been together from June (1809) while Josephine was with Hortense until peace was declared in October. It was the first time that he had actually preferred the company of someone else to Josephine, the first time he had spent more than the occasional hour or day with someone else when he could have had her beside him. Their stay at Finckenstein could have been convenience, but this was deliberate choice.

In guilt and as consolation, he sent Josephine eight hundred shrubs and flowers for her hothouses at Malmaison from the Hapsburg collection at Schönbrunn. Among these were possibly some of the 184 new species that flowered for the first time in France at Malmaison between 1804 and 1814; others came from Egypt and Arabia, blooms that had left the desert air and brought to France an exotic beauty.

Laure Permon was invited to lunch at Malmaison today. She found her hostess melancholy, and complaining 'It is very cold'. But Laure divined: 'It was the chill of grief creeping about her heart.' Josephine begged her to give her details of any conversations she had heard about the 'divorce' between Letizia and Caroline and their followers, and Laure tried to reassure her, saying she had not heard the word once recently. Suddenly Laure's eldest daughter, who was Josephine's godchild and named after her, ran in. All the former fears she had rationally expressed when she said she did not want to bear Napoleon's children now disappeared, and in tears, the Empress said: 'You can have little idea how much I have suffered when any one of you has brought a child to me . . . I struck with barrenness shall be driven in disgrace from the bed of him who has given me a crown. Yet God is my witness that I love him more than my life, and much more than the crown, that crown which he has given me.'

On 22 October Napoleon wrote to Josephine from Munich: 'I am happy at the thought of seeing you and await the moment with impatience. I am leaving within the hour and should arrive at Fontainebleau on the 26th or 27th. You may go there to await my arrival . . .'

Knowing Napoleon, knowing how frantically fast he could travel, losing officers, retinue, even Constant on occasions, Josephine should have known that the shortest calculation would probably be too long. Feeling that divorce was still a possibility, though their perfect six months' had lulled her suspicions, she might have followed her usual punctilious course more closely. But she did not, and when she arrived at Fontainebleau on 26 October, it was to find that Napoleon had already been there for several hours.

He then proceeded to behave with extraordinary callousness, the reasons for which are partly explained by Méneval, his secretary. 'When Napoleon had decided, on his return to Fontainebleau at the end of 1809, to take in hand this grave matter [the divorce] he gave the Empress some hints as to the separation that he was contemplating, a few weeks before the painful sacrifice would have to be consummated. This he did

164 *Napoleon's study at Malmaison: Josephine left it untouched after the divorce*

Librairie Hachette

Josephine retained her title of Empress after the divorce, but Napoleon also made her the Duchess of Navarre – a new duchy created by patent. This portrait by Isabey, who also perfected Josephine's makeup, was painted about 1811, when she was 48

Wallace Coll.

The Battle of Austerlitz, 2 December 1805. Napoleon had calculated the exact
tactics of the Coalition armies against him, and defeated the Russians, Prussians and
Austrians at one stroke. The Czar was in tears

without explaining himself distinctly, and rather by innuendoes calculated to make her reflect than by any explicit remarks. Napoleon, whom many have looked upon as merciless, feared the sight of tears and suffering, which indeed exercised an almost irresistible influence over him . . .'

Rather than face the storms and tears, her sense of natural justice and unnatural loss, therefore, he alleviated his own suffering by increasing hers. For this slow breaking of the news was an extreme torture to Josephine, who, after years of this turbulent and sometimes tormented life had learned to withstand pressure, but was incapable of enduring the long-drawn-out agony of suspense, of tension.

It was a badly planned campaign of attrition, Méneval recorded its phases, which must have struck like a series of electric shocks against the conductor of Josephine's extreme sensibilities: 'An unwonted coldness, the closing of the communications which had up till now remained open between their apartments; the rarity and briefness of the moments which the Emperor vouchsafed to her; some passing storms, though provoked by the slightest pretexts, which troubled this usually peaceable household; the arrival in succession of the allied sovereigns, whose presence she sought in vain to interpret.'

Instead of understanding that sentence of death had been passed by Napoleon upon his heart, and resigning herself to the inevitable consequence, their separation (for he could never resist her in her presence), Josephine became frantic in her torment, like a rabbit caught in a snare, worsening the thing it can neither understand nor escape.

'Her anxiety reached its highest pitch,' says Méneval. 'This state of affairs was too acute to last long; it had introduced into their daily intercourse a constraint which was a torment to them both.'

But it was five weeks before Napoleon could bring himself to be explicit. First the High Chancellor, Cambacérès, was approached as a possible intermediary. He found Napoleon 'striding up and down in the midst of his glory', but refused to be intimidated. He would neither accept the task of breaking the news to the Empress, nor the necessity of a divorce at all.

Napoleon dismissed him, and summoned instead M. de Lavalette, the husband of one of Josephine's Beauharnais nieces. He was equally unwilling to be the messenger, but listened while Napoleon explained the necessity of sacrificing his affections for France, and his reason for not being able to name Eugène as his successor: he was not young enough (Napoleon was now forty, and Eugène twenty-nine).

'At last,' said Méneval, 'the Emperor could hold out no longer.' It was Thursday, 30 November 1809. The couple sat down to dinner. According to Bausset, the Palace Chamberlain, Josephine was looking 'the image of sorrow and despair' in a large white hat, tied under the chin, which hid part of her face: nevertheless he thought that she had been crying and was still on the verge of tears. The silence of the meal, which lasted only about ten minutes instead of the usual fifteen or so, was broken only when Napoleon asked Bausset 'What sort of weather is it?' After dinner he rose, followed slowly by Josephine, and took the coffee handed to him by a page. He signalled that he wished to be alone with her in the drawing room. Bausset withdrew, and sat down in an armchair outside – as near as possible to the door, one may be sure. Next he heard loud screams from Josephine, and an usher rushed to the door, thinking she was ill, but was prevented from opening it by Bausset, who said 'the Emperor would call for assistance if he thought it advisable'.

He himself went and stood outside the door. A few seconds later Napoleon opened it and said sharply 'Come in Bausset, and shut the door'. Bausset continued: 'I entered the room and perceived the Empress lying full length on the carpet, and uttering heartrending cries and lamentations – "No, I shall never survive it".'

Napoleon asked Bausset if he was strong enough to help him carry the Empress down the inner staircase to her own apartments, and between them they struggled down the winding staircase with her. At one moment Josephine whispered to Bausset 'You are holding me too tight', and he ceased to worry so much about her. But now he saw that Napoleon's 'agitation and discomposure were extreme', as was

170

clear from the fact that the Emperor now unburdened himself desperately, 'The interests of France and of my dynasty have done violence to my affections . . . divorce has become a stern duty for me . . . I pity her from the bottom of my heart but I thought she had more character . . . and I was not prepared for such an outburst of grief.' He had to take a long breath between each phrase, his words were almost incoherent, and his eyes were wet with tears. 'The whole scene,' concluded Bausset, recording one of those nuances which bear the true Napoleonic seal, 'did not last more than seven or eight minutes.'

Months of pleasure and weeks of pain could have been avoided if Napoleon had been able to bring himself to a decision after his conversation with Talleyrand some eighteen months before. Even now Josephine had interrupted his round-about explanation, of how he loved her, how he owed all his happiness to her, but how his destiny could not be controlled by his own wishes, with a brave 'Do not say any more. I understand, I expected this, but the blow is none the less mortal'. Then she broke down.

The blow was in fact worse for having fallen so slowly and inexorably, just as an expected knock on the door is the one that causes a start.

But Hortense rushed to comfort her mother with some of that affectionate wisdom of hers: 'We will go with you. I know my brother will feel as I do. For the first time in our lives, far from the world and the court, in some peaceful retreat, we will live a real family life and know our first real happiness.'

Perhaps perceiving the truth of this, particularly as far as her daughter was concerned, Josephine grew calmer; but not Napoleon, whom Hortense had to face next. She told him that after thirteen years of marriage such a scene had hardly been surprising; but when they left she said, 'we will take with us the remembrance of your kindness'. Napoleon had long treated both Hortense and Eugène with as much affection as if he had been their own father, and as a man who invariably hoped to have the best of all worlds, her near-dismissal brought tears to his eyes. With a sob in his throat he cried, 'What? You are all going to abandon me? You no longer love me? Had it merely been a question of my personal happiness, I would have sacrificed that. But the happiness and welfare of France are at stake. You should feel sorry for me, for I am about to renounce all that is dearest to me in this world . . .'

Hortense was not able to resist his tears, any more than he could resist Josephine's, and she was moved: but she refused his threat-or-promise remarks guaranteeing the future of her children and repeated that her duty now lay with her mother.

Eugène arrived within a week, and although Napoleon continued to insist that Josephine would lose neither her position nor his affection, he agreed with Hortense that the break should be complete. 'My sister and I would find ourselves in a false and embarrassing position if we remained at court,' he said.

Napoleon now threw his last two cards into the campaign: 'I need you,' he declared. 'Nor is it your mother's wish that you should separate yourselves and your children from me. Were you to leave me, it might well appear that your mother had been repudiated, perhaps for some just cause.'

This argument, added to the fact that Josephine wished them all to stay as united as possible – she wanted to stay in France, and she wanted to be near Napoleon, as well as her children, thus for her it was the most feasible solution – at last convinced them.

One of the natural worries she had now was about Eugène's future: if Napoleon had his own heir this would be affected. She was not interested in being given any kingdoms herself, but asked for one for Eugène. However, he quickly scotched the idea: he was not going to benefit by his mother's misfortune. The terms of the divorce settlement therefore came down to geographical and financial arrangements. Josephine was to be given Malmaison and the Elysée Palace, to retain the rank and title of 'Queen and Empress' (and, unfortunately, the pomp this required) and to have an allowance of three million francs a year, out of which her current debts of nearly two million francs were to be met forthwith.

The social pressures on her were intensified during the sixteen days which it took to make and finalize all the arrangements. The cruellest moment for her (and one that shows the astonishing lengths to which Napoleon was prepared to go in the minutest details) came at a ball given by the City of Paris on 4 December. Laure Permon was astonished to hear, on arriving, that Napoleon had given orders for Josephine's ladies-in-waiting and the others to go up ahead, instead of waiting for the Empress's arrival. He himself escorted his sister Caroline, the Queen of Naples. Josephine must have felt like a wounded doe when she entered the assembly alone, yet she managed to reach her seat still smiling, though once there she sank down on it, trembling and almost past endurance.

If this was Napoleon's way of testing public opinion on the idea of a divorce (as those who knew him best assumed), it was no wonder that Eugène's first words to Hortense had been 'Has our mother the courage to face this ordeal?' Hortense had rightly replied 'Yes'.

Josephine made her last public appearance in her present role on 14 December 1809, at a reception at the Tuileries, the palace which had always depressed her, and one spectator was moved to write down his feelings about her 'flawless demeanour, in the middle of a court fully conscious that she was making her last appearance...'

Her last private appearance was on 15 December when the process of divorce, which had to be ratified by the Senate, was formally set in motion. She wore an unadorned white dress, and she heard Napoleon say:

> God knows how much it has cost my heart to take such a decision. But there is no sacrifice beyond my courage... I must add that, far from ever having reason for complaint, I can on the contrary only congratulate myself on the affection and tenderness of my well-beloved wife. She has embellished fifteen [sic] years of my life; the memory of this will be for ever graven on my heart. She has been crowned by my hand; it is my desire that she should retain the rank and title of Crowned Empress, but above all that she should never doubt my affection and that she should always regard me as her best and dearest friend.

Josephine started to read her own speech: 'With the permission of my august and dear husband, I have to declare that having no longer any hope of bearing children who could fulfil the needs of his policies and the interest of France, I am pleased to offer him the greatest proof of attachment and devotion that has ever been given on this earth . . .' She began to sob, and Regnault took the text from her to finish reading it aloud.

Josephine's reply had also been written by Napoleon. Their original civil marriage had been dissolved 'by mutual consent'; (although she was forty-six, and therefore these grounds were not legally good) and the religious ceremony that had been performed on the eve of the Coronation, five years before, was speedily annulled, not by the Pope, who had excommunicated Napoleon after the Emperor had seized the Holy Roman Empire and was now himself held prisoner, but by a tribunal, on the grounds that it had lacked the proper priest and witnesses. So Josephine's secret ceremony had not saved her marriage after all, though *perhaps* it saved her life.

On 16 December the Paris newspaper *Le Moniteur* carried a report of the public divorce and noted 'The Emperor wept'.

On 16 December Josephine set out for the last time from the Tuileries to go to Malmaison.

Talleyrand, who had been a witness at the secret marriage ceremony and then not a witness when witnesses were decreed *de trop,* told Claire de Rémusat: 'There is no one in the palace who will not regret the day she goes. She is gentle, sweet and kind, and she knows how to calm the Emperor. She understands everyone's problems here, and has been a refuge to us all a thousand times. When some foreign princess arrives to take her place, you will see friction between the Emperor and the courtiers. We will all be the losers by it.'

The straightforward, frank little Mlle Georges, now twenty-two years old and living in St Petersburg, far from fear or favour of Napoleon, wrote simply: 'What a misfortune for France and for the Emperor.'

10. Peace and Politics

Josephine left the Tuileries in the rain. She was heavily veiled and did not look behind her. It was still raining when the carriage lumbered up the drive to Malmaison – only ten miles away, and yet now, for her, a different world. She would soon find that many of the ladies who had spent the morning weeping in her apartments at the Tuileries would find it quite impossible to visit her at Malmaison.

For the moment, on that desolate December day, she busied herself with settling in the pets she had brought with her in the carriage: a parrot, and a pair of wolfhounds, together with a basketful of their puppies. Malmaison, essentially a spring and summer paradise, a place for Josephine's private love and family simplicity, must now have seemed dank and drear. She felt deeply depressed, yet was too agitated to sleep. Mlle Avrillon stayed with her and they talked through the night.

It was little better with Napoleon. About one and a half hours after she had left the Tuileries, he had set off for Versailles, which was also empty and echoing in the rain. The Bonapartes, no longer making any attempt to hide their air of triumph, soon found they could not raise his spirits with games of cards or any other suggestions. Napoleon was to remain totally downcast for a week, shut up alone in his apartments for much of the time. He was mourning not only the woman who would have had the ability to change his moods, but also the loss of the best part of his life and, in a sense, of himself: Josephine had seen him at his most imaginative, sensitive, helpful and sweet, as well as at his most passionate. With no one to know and demand this side of his nature now, it would soon die away.

On 17 December, the day after they had parted (Josephine had fainted at the Tuileries when Napoleon, accompanied by Méneval, went in to say goodbye to her), Napoleon could bear it no longer: he ordered his carriage and drove over from the Trianon at Versailles to Malmaison. She saw his carriage coming and went down into the courtyard to await him. Then, careful to keep in sight of everyone but out of earshot, they walked hand in hand together in the rain. That night the

Emperor wrote to Josephine:

My dear, I found you weaker than you should be. You have shown courage. You must find more to sustain you; you must not allow yourself to sink into depression; you must cheer yourself up and above all take care of your health, which is so precious to me. If you care for me, if you love me, you must be strong and make yourself happy. You cannot doubt my constant and tender affection, and you would make a great mistake about my feelings for you if you thought I could be happy if you are not happy, or content if you are not calm. Adieu, my friend; sleep well; remember that I wish it.

Letters did not cease to flow from him, sometimes at the rate of two a day, and tears did not cease to flow from Josephine. Claire de Rémusat, one of those who had sufficient decency to remain, for a while at least, faithful to her Empress, noticed that when the letters were delivered late in the day they caused Josephine still worse nights, and hinted to the Emperor that he should write less often. With Josephine too, she was practical, encouraging her to take walks in the grounds, trying to tempt her to a revived interest in anything: her gardens, her plans for the spring blooms, her indoor games. But without Napoleon at Malmaison, Josephine felt disorientated and disembodied there. 'Sometimes,' she told Claire, 'I feel as if I am dead and that all that remains is a sort of vague realization that I no longer exist.'

On Christmas Day, Napoleon invited her to dine with him at the Trianon, in the company of Eugène, Hortense and Caroline. Mlle Avrillon noted that the Empress came home so elated that it was hard to believe they were divorced; and certainly nobody every heard a word of reproach cross her lips. Even the tough-minded Claire was eventually moved to a tribute: 'She is truly as sweet as an angel.'

Her position was of course doubly difficult because her divorce certainly did not give her freedom. She was still completely dependent, financially, geographically, and particularly through her vulnerability on behalf of her children

176

and grandchildren, on the most powerful and terrifying man in Europe. She was still watched and probably had expected this. Fear as well as love, therefore, must have played some part in her emotions at this time, though she may not have realized that this was so.

When the chance for a small degree of independence was offered again, however, she refused it. It came in the form of an offer of marriage from Crown Prince Frederick, who had never forgotten the charms of her company two years before. Napoleon urged her to accept him, but she would not. Another much younger man, a relative, Maurice de Tascher, found her 'still beautiful and seductive': like Shakespeare's Cleopatra, she had a quality that defied age.

She was, after all, only forty-six; but in comparison with the brides Napoleon had been considering for political purposes, that was indeed a grandmotherly age. The fourteen-year-old Archduchess of Russia had not been promised quickly enough for Napoleon's taste, so he had put in a proposal instead for the eighteen-year-old Archduchess Marie-Louise of Austria – even before he had obtained his divorce from Josephine.

Now, in the New Year of 1810, Metternich's wife visited Malmaison and was astonished to find that the Empress wanted her to help to arrange her ex-husband's marriage to his new Empress. Her report on this to her husband drew from Metternich himself a new accolade for Josephine's 'strength of character': previously he had been full of admiration for her ability to outwit the subterfuges of the Bonapartes.

Presents were pouring into Malmaison from the Emperor. He sent Josephine game whenever he hunted, and gifts, and an extra 100,000 francs to 'plant whatever you like'. Then in March, when his proxy marriage with Marie-Louise took place in Vienna, he sent Josephine details of a new possession: the chateau and duchy of Navarre in Normandy. He had had the duchy specially created for her by patent. There was also a letter, which said, 'You should go on 25 March and arrange to spend the month of April there.' Evidently he felt that two Empresses of France should not be living within ten miles of one another, although from various later remarks of

Josephine's he seems also to have retained a romantic notion that they might all become friends, that he could keep the previous wife for companionship and the new one for having children. Josephine later said she would have agreed to meeting Marie-Louise only to please the Emperor. However, she did not have to make the decision, for if the much more mature Josephine no longer suffered from jealousy, Napoleon's new wife had to contend with the image of a fascinating woman who, as the whole of Europe knew, had dominated her husband for years, and whom he still regretted leaving. It was she, therefore, who refused to meet Josephine.

Napoleon had gone to meet his new wife at Compiègne. On seeing her he ascertained that the proxy marriage was valid, and then lost no time in making it more so by consummating it on the spot. He seemed very pleased with his new bride, whom he considered as 'fresh as roses' (later the image would be turned into 'an abyss covered with flowers', but that was still far ahead); but as she liked her rooms, even her bedroom, icy cold, and he liked fires even in July, he did not spend as much time with her as he had done with Josephine. However, he was a naturally uxorious and despotic man, wrote to Marie-Louise very affectionately on most days when they were apart, and, of course, had her watched.

Without any doubt, the worst of Josephine's trials were over. Having lost that which she dreaded losing, she gradually began to feel the tranquillity of those who, after intense suffering, attain a respite in which pleasure consists of not knowing pain.

And after this came genuine enjoyment.

But there were pinpricks. Josephine, though she had never known envy (the blight of the Bonapartes) and had outgrown jealousy, still retained the real ghost of her childhood, which each experience since had magnified: insecurity. Many of her household had now deserted to Marie-Louise. She had spent a few weeks at the Elysée Palace in Paris before leaving for Normandy, and had found herself largely overlooked in the capital; now she found Navarre in a run-down, rotting, damp condition, with too much water even in the garden. Knowing

*Napoleon drove out through
Soissons, near Compiègne, to
meet Marie-Louise incognito,
but was recognized and drove
back with her in her coach*

*Marie-Louise of Austria,
Napoleon's second Empress*

Napoleon as she did, knowing how each move could be
calculated in a war of nerves, she wondered: was it all
deliberate? Was she to be exiled from Malmaison and kept in
misery far from the place she thought of as home?

She carried out her searching enquiries through Eugène, and
was partly reassured. As a result, she wrote to Napoleon on
19 April (1810), for the first and only time as a subject might:

Sire,

Through my son, I have received an assurance that Your
Majesty consents to my return to Malmaison, and that you
agree to give me the advances which I have requested to

179

make the Château of Navarre habitable. This double favour, Sire, largely removes the anxieties, even fears, aroused in me by your Majesty's long silence.

... Your Majesty can rest assured that even when I am in residence at Malmaison I shall live as if I were a thousand leagues from Paris. I have made a great sacrifice Sire, and every day I realize even more its extent. However this sacrifice will be as it should; conclusive on my part. Your Majesty will not find your good fortune troubled by any word of my regrets...

I limit myself to asking one favour, that you will deign sometimes to find a way to reassure me and those about me that I will always have a little place in your memory and a large place in your regard and affections...

Napoleon replied:

My dear,

I have received your letter of April 19. It is in a bad style. My feelings do not change. I don't know what Eugène can have said to you. I didn't write to you because you didn't write, and I wanted to do everything that would please you.

I note with pleasure that you are going to Malmaison and will be happy there... I shall say no more until you have compared this letter with yours, and after that I leave you to judge who is the better friend – you or me. Adieu my friend, stay well and be fair, both to yourself and to me.

She was happy again, though any contact with Napoleon partly reopened the wound, as when he arrived one June morning unexpectedly at Malmaison at ten o'clock in the morning. Fortunately Josephine was already up and in the garden. They embraced, and, according to one footman, both wept; although in a letter to Hortense Josephine said she had kept the tears back till he left.

Hortense's life was still following the same terrible pattern with Louis. She had left him once, to be ordered back soon afterwards by Napoleon; now a doctor's diagnosis of tuberculosis and depression allowed her to escape him once more and go to Plombières; Josephine promised to share her last possession with her so that she could choose her own fate at least in so far as financial independence could improve her desperate situation.

One of Hortense's letters, talking of death, had shaken Josephine badly. But in July, good news followed: Louis had been unable to accept all Napoleon's plans for a European trading scheme excluding Britain, which he felt would not be beneficial for the Dutch, and where Hortense was not concerned he remained a just man. He abdicated. Even Napoleon admitted that Hortense was now free to do as she liked: and she travelled from Plombières to join Josephine for a wonderful summer in Aix-les-Bains.

The month from late July on was 'the happiest month of my whole life' for Hortense, who was there with Colonel Charles de Flahaut, the lover into whose arms Louis's insensate jealousy had finally and almost inevitably driven her. It was a happy summer too for Josephine, who was also visited twice by Eugène. In the autumn, finding it better now to keep on the move, she went to Switzerland, and from there, hearing that Marie-Louise was pregnant and obviously wanting to put Napoleon at his ease about her own reaction to this, she wrote to him.

He replied, 'Yes, the Empress is in her fourth month of pregnancy. She is feeling well and is very fond of me.'

From Claire de Rémusat came more ominous news: the Emperor had been driving near Malmaison (while Josephine was in Switzerland) and had offered to show it to Marie-Louise: she had not replied but her eyes had filled with tears. Claire analysed the pregnant girl's jealousy, and concluded, 'Were your personal charms less striking, your role today might be less difficult.' She suggested that a return to Malmaison would be far too close for Marie-Louise's comfort, and that in time even Navarre might not be distant enough.

Josephine was stung. Was she to lose her home as well as her husband and many of her household? She truly dreaded exile. With a noticeable touch of asperity, a sign too of her improved mental health, she wrote sharply: 'Bonaparte, you promised you would never abandon me. Now I find myself in a position in which I need your advice. Talk to me frankly. May I return to Paris or must I stay away?' He could reply either by letter, or through Hortense who now had to return to Court, and who had an audience with Napoleon at Fontainebleau.

Hortense could see that he would be relieved if Josephine herself offered to stay in Italy with Eugène. He explained: 'I must think of my wife's happiness. Things have not turned out as I had hoped they would. She resents... the influence your mother is known to exercise over me. In spite of all this, I shall never agree to constrain the Empress Josephine in any way.' (He did, however, throw in some bait about kingdoms, governorships, and so on, apparently unable in her absence to remember precisely how different Josephine's aspirations were from those of his own clan). Josephine waited for the news in a fever. Most of her household were homesick too, and she felt they would resign if they were forced to spend even the winter in Italy.

At last a definite answer came: permission to return to Navarre, which had now been restored and made sufficiently comfortable. Josephine's household was in a delirium of joy: and from now on she was to enjoy the tranquillity of an ordered and simple country life.

Her excruciating headaches, her literal crown of thorns at Court, vanished completely. The tears which had once seemed an inevitable part of daily life, found no fresh excuses to flow: 'I only cry occasionally now,' she wrote to Hortense. To Claire, who was enjoying the quiet winter now that central heating had been installed, she said serenely: 'Peace of mind is a substitute for happiness.'

The sharp-eyed Claire noted that Josephine seemed genuinely contented. Others were astonished that her slender frame, no doubt kept thin by constant anxiety during the years at Court, was now filling out, reports of which made Napoleon write 'I hear you are as plump as a good Normandy farmer's wife'.

At last Josephine, well aware that her air of sorrow had

suited her, was forced to admit the truth herself: 'No longer being Empress seems to agree with me.'

Her days as Duchess of Navarre were full, not with the frantic engagements and changes of plans of the days at Court, but with a restful order. Embroidery, listening to books being read aloud, planning the gardens, the indoor games, from cards to billiards, that she had always played so well, and outside, drives in the parks and forests, fishing, and in winter skating, with some of the ladies using improvised armchairs on skates. (When one of them went through the ice and broke a leg, Josephine visited her in bed every day for two months.)

There were some visitors: those who were ordered to call by Napoleon, and those who came out of curiosity or genuine friendship, including the elderly but cheerful Bishop of Evreux, with whom Josephine played Tric-Trac.

However, any slight slackening of formality was at once reported to Napoleon and censured, as when she went driving in the Normandy forests without her full complement of fourteen troopers and a trumpeter, and allowed the gentlemen of her household to wear simpler uniforms. The Imperial command thundered from Paris, and full Court dress was resumed.

But although she knew that every action and every word was being relayed to the Emperor, Josephine did not impose constraints on conversation, and thus a relaxed, happy household enjoyed with her this rest from what she herself admitted had been the fatiguing ceremony of Court. Even Claire found the company easy-going and agreeable. She added, 'We are always together for, as you know, the Empress does not like being alone.'

On 20 March 1811 the bells rang out to celebrate the birth of Napoleon's son and heir, the King of Rome. Josephine sent her congratulations to Paris at once, and within two days Eugène was with her, bringing a letter from Napoleon: 'My friend, I have received your letter. Thank you. My son is fat and healthy. I hope he will thrive. He has my chest, my mouth and my eyes. I hope he will fulfil his destiny. I am always very pleased with Eugène. He has never given me the slightest

*Napoleon presents the King of Rome, his son, to the dignitaries of the Empire.
The baby is in the arms of his governess, the Countess of Montesquiou; his mother,
the Empress Marie-Louise, is seated on the bed*

worry.' – a graceful touch, as ever, so that she did not feel that
the baby who was disinheriting her son from the kingdom of
Italy was replacing him in the Emperor's regard, and one that
Josephine appreciated at once.

In April (1811) Napoleon gave her permission to return to
Malmaison. There one of her recurrent troubles flared up: her
finances were investigated, and it emerged that some of her
staff had been cheating her, while she herself had been as open-
handed as usual and was again in debt. Mollien, the state
treasurer, was instructed to investigate her monetary affairs and,
no doubt taking his cue from Napoleon's initial anger, over-
stepped the mark and reduced Josephine to tears. Reporting
this (probably proudly) to his master, he received, instead of
praise, a pained 'But you need not have made her cry!' and
Napoleon wrote at once to console her. (Later, Napoleon

himself was to publicly regret the sternness he had shown to Josephine over her debts, which he remembered as their one source of serious disagreement.)

Meanwhile Josephine had sought his help on another project: she wanted to see the King of Rome, and without the knowledge of Marie-Louise Napoleon gave orders for his governess, Mme Montesquiou, to arrange this. An 'accidental' rendezvous took place in the Bois de Boulogne, and Josephine spent an hour with the child and his governess. Then she asked to see his nurse, who said after she left: 'Goodness, this one's nice. She's said more to me in a quarter of an hour than the other one has in six months.'

Hortense was managing to keep on good terms with Marie-Louise, as she was instructed to do by Napoleon, though most of those at court found the new Empress cold and uninspiring. When, in the spring of 1812 Napoleon launched his campaign against Russia, it was to Eugène, not to any of his own family, that he offered the regency of France. Eugène, however, declined; he wanted to see active service again. Meanwhile Josephine was given permission to join Eugène's wife in Milan, where she was expecting their fourth child.

In September (1812) Eugène wrote to Milan to tell them of their apparent but treacherous victory at the Battle of Borodino. He added to his mother: 'I cannot thank you enough for the attentions and kindness you have shown to my little family. You are adored in Milan, as everywhere. People have written charming things about you, and you have turned the head of everyone you have been near.'

The next month she returned to Malmaison by way of Switzerland, and a little estate she had acquired there, just in case Napoleon should insist on her living outside France, which, after her concern for the happiness and security of her children, was now her chief anxiety. The jealousy she had once felt for Marie Walewska had completely vanished now that she no longer had anything to lose (this is interesting, for it shows that Josephine's jealousy was based on her insecurity rather than sexual competitiveness). She now wanted to meet Marie Walewska and Napoleon's son by her, and invited them to

Malmaison. The child had been given the name Walewski by the Count, Marie's husband. Apparently the meeting went well, which shows a new serenity in Josephine's own character.

But public opinion in Paris was restive. Two days before Josephine returned to Malmaison a man called Malet, a former army officer, had announced that the Emperor had been killed in action against the Russians, and he had very nearly succeeded in seizing power. Always sensitive to danger, Josephine became fearful once more and wrote to Eugène: 'Watch carefully over the Emperor's safety, for these evil men are capable of anything. Tell him from me that he is wrong to live in palaces without knowing whether they are mined.'

Though she did not know it yet, only a fraction of Moscow was still standing. Ninety per cent of the houses had been razed to the ground in the Russians' last desperate stand, in which they also burned twenty thousand of their own wounded who were unable to move from their beds. Napoleon turned back and began leading his dispirited and hungry men over the thousands of kilometres which had begun on scorched earth and ended as a frozen wasteland. News, first of the defeat, and then of the misery, began to filter into the French capital, and Parisians wondered: had Napoleon's luck left him, when he put aside *Notre Dame des Victoires?*

For once even Marie-Louise was jolted out of her insularity and felt enough pity for Josephine's frantic concern to show Napoleon's letters to Hortense, knowing that any news from him would be passed on to comfort her mother. At last, on 18 December, the Emperor rode back into Paris: although it was midnight, he immediately sent word to Josephine that he was safe. Soon afterwards he went in person to tell her about the campaign, and to show that he was well. It must have been, for all the pleasure of being together again, one of their least joyful and hopeful meetings. It was also their last.

Hortense had spoken with insight when she promised her mother their first really happy family life together, away from the Court. The next summer (1813) passed more pleasantly for Josephine at Malmaison (where she had her two Bonaparte grandsons staying with her while Hortense was at Plombières) than it might have done in the strained surroundings of Court. Everywhere now there were small signs that people were only awaiting the right opportunity to turn their coats and loyalty away from the Emperor: but Josephine was absorbed in the activities of these two small boys, the younger of whom, the five-year-old Charles-Louis-Napoleon, had his heart's greatest wish granted when he was allowed to run around in the mud like the boys of the village. Josephine wrote telling Hortense that she was following her instructions for their diet and studies to the letter, which was not entirely true as the future Napoleon III looked back on this time with relish as a holiday on which he had been thoroughly spoiled by his grandmother.

So it was still at Malmaison that Josephine found her greatest pleasure. But now, rather than in the wonderfully planted gardens or the recently extended art gallery which housed a magnificent and catholic collection – her architects had extended the gallery to a hundred feet in 1809, and even this must have been small for a collector as eclectic as Josephine – she was revelling in the nursery and the playroom, or among the sugar canes which the little boys loved to cut down. 'They enliven everything about me,' she told her daughter. 'You see how happy you have made me by leaving them with me.'

In August (1813) came evidence that Napoleon's marriage had not achieved its political ends: his father-in-law, Francis I of Austria, joined the Allies against Napoleon. In October came the great defeat at Leipzig that presaged his downfall. The Crown Prince of Sweden, Bernadotte, a former marshal of France who had, with a little help from the Emperor, married Napoleon's 'first love' Desirée, turned against him, and Murat, the King of Naples, was on the verge of following suit. The Confederation of the Rhine was dissolving into enmity. Joseph had fled from Spain.

Yet Louis wrote to ask to be allowed to return to France and serve his brother, which won him back Hortense's respect, even though she could no longer hope to love him. And when, at the end of November (1812), Eugène's father-in-law, the King of Bavaria, promised him a crown if he would desert Napoleon, Eugène replied with grace and strength, thus preserving the Beauharnais unity: 'It is not to be denied that the Emperor's star is beginning to wane, but this is only one additional reason why those who have received benefits from him should remain loyal to him.' Eugène also wrote to Napoleon, telling him that in his opinion the King of Bavaria would prefer a son-in-law who was an honest if a simple man, than one who was a king and a traitor. His wife stood by his decision and severed communications with her family.

Josephine waited and worried at Malmaison. She and her ladies, 'guarded' by a handful of wounded grenadiers and veterans, had answered a request for lint from the nursing sisters by starting to make their own. Napoleon fought his way back to France in November and told the Senate: 'The Great Empire no longer exists. It is France we must now defend.' He sent Méneval to Malmaison with the message that Josephine was not to be frightened.

Then, just before Christmas (1813), the Allies began to cross the Rhine, and as they encroached further on French soil, panic seized the people of Paris. In March (1814) Napoleon left Joseph to defend the capital and himself went to command the defence from Fontainebleau; on 29 March Marie-Louise left for Blois, accompanied, on Louis's orders, by Hortense. Hortense herself gave orders to Josephine: she was to go at once to Navarre, and there she went, with her best diamonds sewn inside her skirts by Mlle Avrillon, still sure that the Emperor would come at the last minute to save Paris, and that Eugène would be in time to back him with troops from Italy, as she had written, at Napoleon's behest, imploring him to do, on 9 February. 'Come quickly,' she had written, but not even Beauharnais loyalty could cover the miles in time to beat the Allies, who arrived at the gates of Paris on 30 March to find General Marmont, another of Napoleon's oldest campaigners, ready to hand the capital over to them together with his own services. And Talleyrand was paid for his treachery by being made head of the new provisional government.

On 31 March Czar Alexander led the Allied monarchs and troops into Paris. Napoleon's suggestion that he should abdicate in favour of the King of Rome, his son, was eventually turned down, at Talleyrand's instigation. Napoleon abdicated on 6 April 1814; but he knew now that he would be succeeded by a restored Bourbon monarch, by Louis XVIII, with whom he had earlier refused to treat.

On the day of the Allies' entry into Paris, Josephine wrote to Hortense: 'I have never lacked the courage to meet the many dangerous situations in which I have found myself throughout my life, and I should always be able to face reversals of fortune with calm, but what I cannot bear is this separation from my children, this uncertainty about their fate. I haven't stopped crying for two days. Send me news of yourself and your children – and of Eugène and his family, if you hear from them...'

On hearing of the abdication she wrote to Eugène: 'How I have suffered at the way in which they have treated the Emperor! What attacks in the newspapers, what ingratitude on the part of those upon whom he showered his favours! . . . as for you, you are free, and absolved from any oath of fidelity.'

The Beauharnais family would never cease in their united love and support of the man they had grown to love as husband and father, but Napoleon himself had written to Josephine that she should now try to obtain the best possible treatment and terms for her family from the Allies: as a member of the *ancien régime* aristocracy and as an Empress who had been divorced by their enemy, they would have little against her if she showed herself realistically conciliatory.

A few days later the Treaty of Fontainebleau was signed. Josephine, as Napoleon had asked the Allies, was to receive a pension of one million francs: though only a third of her previous allowance, it was generous. Provision was to be made for Hortense and Eugène. Napoleon, according to some sources, tried to poison himself on the eve of the signature of the Treaty: he certainly always carried a phial of poison with him, and suicide had been an adolescent preoccupation of his, but if it was a serious attempt it was remarkably unsuccessful for such a thorough man. Allegedly, he told Caulaincourt, 'Tell Josephine I was thinking of her until the moment I died.'

Then, from Fontainebleau, he wrote to her:

> In retirement I shall substitute the pen for the sword . . .
> They have betrayed me, yes, all of them. I except only our dear Eugène, so worthy of you and me.
> Adieu my dear Josephine. Resign yourself, as I am doing, and always remember someone who has never forgotten you, and never will forget you . . . I shall await news of you at Elba. My health is not good.

Marie-Louise had taken the King of Rome to Rambouillet. Hortense went to see her and express her continued loyalty, but was dismissed by the Empress, who inadvertently lost the support of Hortense when she blurted out in fright 'Do you think my father will make me go to the island of Elba?' (He did not, and the King of Rome was kept in virtual captivity in Vienna until his death.) According to both Hortense and Laure Permon, Josephine's reaction was the opposite, and she was shocked at her successor's disloyalty: only fear of preventing a reconciliation which she knew Napoleon still desired with Marie-Louise prevented her from going to Elba at once. 'And I believe she would have done it,' said Napoleon when he was told of this later.

Meanwhile on 14 April she returned to Malmaison, where a Russian guard was protecting her treasures. The next day, Czar Alexander called on her, having first politely made sure he would not be unwelcome. Hortense, arriving soon afterwards, was shaken to find her mother walking in the garden arm in arm with the most powerful man among the Allies. She and Eugène never acquired the degree of political sophistication that came naturally to Napoleon and had been acquired by Josephine in a lifetime of surviving continually opposed exigencies, for which she now had Napoleon's own persuasive argument, 'The future of your children depends on it.'

'Here are my daughter and her sons. I recommend them to your protection,' she now said simply to Alexander, and afterwards privately reproved Hortense for her chilliness in the face of a past enemy who had now promised to be their

Napoleon in 1814, the year of Josephine's death

protector, and who had won better terms for Napoleon himself than others had proposed.

Germaine de Staël, quick as ever to pry into interesting situations, arrived at Malmaison to ply Josephine with questions in the long picture gallery. For once the gentle Josephine was forced to be abrupt, and returned to the salon from the encounter 'visibly unstrung'. She unburdened herself to another guest: 'Mme de Staël had the effrontery to ask me whether I still loved the Emperor! As if I could feel less keenly for him today, in his misfortune – I who never stopped loving the Emperor in the days of his good luck!' Here was the truth. She no longer had anything to fear from Bonaparte; she was no longer in any way, except in her willing heart, '*His* Josephine'. He no longer had power or dominion over her. It had perhaps been harder to be sure that she loved him when so much depended on his favour; but now she and the world could be sure. It *was* love she felt.

A letter came from Czar Alexander, who had fallen at once under the spell of this woman who had suffered and survived so much – survived with her family honour intact, her heart and her charm still matchless, yet still vulnerable. 'It was with the keenest regret that I saw your Majesty still had some anxieties... Though I do not wish to exploit the permission you have been kind enough to give me, Madame, I look forward to presenting my respects to you on Friday at your dinner hour.'

Josephine ordered new dresses from Leroy that cost 6,000 francs, and prepared for her last campaign, to ensure the future and security of Hortense, Eugène and her grandchildren.

A month later, on 15 May, while Alexander was on a two-day visit to Hortense's château of St Leu, Josephine caught a chill driving in an open carriage through the forest. She retired and confessed her deepest anxieties to a confidant: 'I can't throw off this terrible depression . . . I'm beginning to lose hope. The Czar Alexander's intentions are the best, but as yet nothing definite has been achieved... those in Paris are unlikely to carry them out once he has left. I have suffered enough already at the fate of the Emperor Napoleon...Must I now see my children penniless wanderers?'

Ten days later, still ill, she opened a ball for the Russian visitors by dancing with Alexander. Then, wearing one of her new ravishing flimsy gowns, without even one of her beloved cashmere shawls, she went out with him from the over-heated ballroom to take the night air, scented with lilies of the valley and lilacs beneath the full-blooming chestnut trees.

The next day she was feverish and her throat badly inflamed; but she received visitors. On Friday 27 May Alexander was expected to dinner again. Hortense told her mother that he could not keep the engagement, and saw him alone. Her mother feared: 'Perhaps he is embarrassed at still having nothing to report to us on the progress of our affairs.' Later that night the Czar sent his personal physician to see her; he was joined the next day by two doctors from Paris who saw that her condition was critical.

Josephine would not allow her grandsons to enter the room, in case her illness were contagious; for the same reason she forfeited seeing some new sketches which Redouté, who was preparing one of his great books on the Malmaison flowers, wanted to show her himself.

Eugène had collapsed under the strain of watching his mother's decline and was ill in bed himself. However, by Monday 29 May he was on his feet beside her and it was Hortense, who, anguished that her mother held out her arms to them that morning but could no longer speak distinctly, fell prostrate, and was gently sent out by her brother.

The last rites were administered.

At noon, Josephine, in the arms of a son who loved his mother as much as anyone on earth, 'went as gently and sweetly to meet death as she had met life'.

She was fifty, and had died from a throat infection aggravated, her physician believed and later told Napoleon, by grief and her anxieties about the fate of the Emperor and of her children. She was not the direct victim of a 'violent commotion', as Marie-Antoinette had been, but she was killed by her own anxious heart.

Her children were too grieved to attend her funeral or even to notify Napoleon, who heard the news accidentally on Elba when one of his valets returned with a newspaper cutting. There, one of his entourage noted, 'He appeared greatly afflicted. He shut himself up within, and would see no one but his grand marshal.'

During his hundred days' escape from Elba in 1815, Napoleon returned to Malmaison and asked Hortense, who had not been back there, to accompany him. 'Every minute I expect to see her coming down one of the garden paths, gathering the flowers she loved so much,' he said. He preferred to go alone up to Josephine's bedroom, and returned from it with wet eyes.

Years later, during his long exile on St Helena, he recalled that she 'had the sweetest little backside in the world. On it you could see the three islets of Martinique.' Though illness, bitterness and depression took their toll, he remained moved by the thought of her 'devotion and absolute self-sacrifice'. He said she had brought her husband great happiness and 'was always his tenderest friend'.

And even when, in a mood of black desolation, he was brooding on her faults, he said 'I really loved her ... She had something, I don't know what, that attracted me. She was a real woman.'

INDEX

195